Together and A

Together and Apart

A Memoir of the Religious Life

Ellen Stephen, OSH

MOREHOUSE PUBLISHING
an imprint of Church Publishing Incorporated
Harrisburg ⁓ New York

Unless otherwise noted, the Scripture quotations contained herein are
from the *New Revised Standard Version Bible,* copyright © 1989 by the
Division of Christian Education of the National Council of Churches of
Christ in the U.S.A. Used by permission. All rights reserved.

Library of Congress Cataloging-in-Publication Data
Stephen, Ellen, 1930–
Together and apart : a memoir of the religious life / Ellen Stephen.
        p.   cm.
ISBN 978-0-8192-2315-9 (pbk.)
1. Monastic and religious life of women. 2. Stephen, Ellen, 1930–
3. Order of St. Helena. I. Title.
BX5974.S74A3 2008
271'.983—dc22

                                    2008021367

Printed in the United States of America.

Cover image: The chapel at the Convent of St. Helena in Vails Gate,
New York, by the Reverend Claire Lofgren
Cover design: Brenda Klinger
Interior design: Vicki K. Black
Author photo: Jane Collin

Morehouse Publishing
4775 Linglestown Road
Harrisburg, PA 17112

Morehouse Publishing
445 Fifth Avenue
New York, NY 10016

Morehouse Publishing is an imprint of Church Publishing Incorporated.

08 09 10 11 12 13   10 9 8 7 6 5 4 3 2 1

Ad Majorem Dei Gloriam

And to all the good people
who have inspired, taught, and companioned me
toward and on the road that leads to life.

Contents

Acknowledgments

I am extremely grateful to my sisters in the Order of Saint Helena, past and present, for being a community in which I have been challenged and supported, and in which I find my calling and my joy.

I cannot thank my editor, Cynthia Shattuck, enough for her skill, directness, and encouragement. Without her, this would not be the book it is.

I thank the early readers of this manuscript for their affirmation and helpful critiques, especially the Reverend Nancy Roth, who introduced me and my manuscript to Cynthia Shattuck.

I also acknowledge with great thankfulness all those who have written of the life of the spirit, and whose wisdom has shaped and informed both my life and my own writing.

Finally, I thank my loving God, my "significant other," for unfailing guidance and presence in my life.

CHAPTER ONE

The Eyes of the Body

The religious life has traditionally used the terms *father, mother, sister,* and *brother,* but it is not a family. It uses the term *community,* but it is not a neighborhood or a village. Although it has often had hierarchical structures such as boards and councils, which may resemble those of secular organizations, it is not a business. It seeks to nurture psychological maturity in its members, but it is not a therapeutic society. Some religious communities emphasize study and teaching, but the religious life is not, in itself, an academic institution. Other religious orders work against the evils of ignorance and injustice, but they are not, except in metaphor, an army. The purpose of the religious life is to praise and serve God, but it is not a church.

What, then, is a religious community? How is the choice for the religious life made, and what lies behind the vows of poverty, chastity, and obedience? What are the nuts and bolts of monastic calling, and why do monks and nuns live as they do? Is this lifestyle appropriate for people today and, if so, how may it be lived in the modern world? These are some of the questions I hope to raise and answer in this book from the perspective of more than forty years in an Anglican religious community.

The themes of coming together and drawing apart are two main characteristics of the religious life. Within most of the major spiritual traditions there have always been communities of people who feel a call to set themselves apart from the prevailing culture. Sometimes this involves a geographical move to the mountains or the desert; almost always it is an inner movement toward the search for truth. A going apart from society to get one's bearings has often been felt as a wake-up call, and may result in a change of one's life direction. Such a choice has variously been called a vocation to the inner way, the way of the Tao, the "examined life," the way of Zen, the way of the mystic. The truth-seeker has many names—pilgrim, seer, *staaretz*, elder, shaman, swami, prophet, sheik, nun, monk, and friar, among others. Sometimes the call has been to a solitary life, and sometimes to a community of like-minded persons. Sometimes the vocation can, in time, lead one back from a place apart to a vowed and active life in the heart of society to serve there as a witness to a different way of living.

The call to go apart has ancient roots, and a strong tradition of wilderness spirituality existed before the time of Christ. A desert or a mountain cave is a place of silence and solitude—a place to "hear oneself think." It has been suggested that at the outset of his ministry, when Jesus was driven into the desert by the Holy Spirit, he may have found himself on the very cliffs of the Wadi Qumran that held the caves of the Essenes, and there confronted his call to public ministry. My own "wilderness" was very different. I first heard my call while living in a small studio apartment in the West Village of New York City in the 1960s. I was living alone and studying drama and playwriting. There wasn't much physical space—just one room and a tiny kitchen and bath—and no view to speak of, but there was a lot of silence and inner space for me to think about the current realities and direction of my life. Even though I was in the heart of the city, I felt somehow apart from the main culture of American life.

But a call to the religious life is first and foremost an invitation to be *together*. Whether this call is to a solitary life or to a community, there is always a consciousness of the importance of human relationship, of love. Even hermits have traditionally welcomed and conversed with those who come seeking wisdom, and have often allowed such seekers to live with or near them. The truth-seeker invariably lives and teaches the oneness or "togetherness" of all humanity and indeed all creatures. Most modern communities and even solitary monastics have a number of associates and friends who mutually share prayer and support. Every human being is called in some manner to the love and service of the human community.

Both characteristics of *apart* and *together* are found in the two great commandments:

> "You shall love the Lord your God with all your heart, and with all your soul, and with all your mind." This is the greatest and first commandment. And a second is like it: "You shall love your neighbor as yourself." (Matthew 22:37–39)

These two commandments are crucial to the development of all forms of Christian discipleship and they may be imagined as a cross. The vertical thrust describes the relationship of the individual spirit to the Holy Spirit or Creator; the horizontal dimension represents the relationship of the individual to other people and indeed all creatures.

Of course when I first got the idea that the religious life might have something to do with *my* life, I wasn't thinking of "apart" and "together"—much less about a cross! I had read about the great truth-seekers, and they and their lifestyles seemed to me strangely attractive, but also alien and somewhat off-putting. I began thinking: "Why on earth would anyone want live like that? What is that sort of lifestyle *for*? What good does it do?" And then the questions came closer to home: "Why would I want to live like that? Maybe *after* I write the Great American Poetic Drama, when I'm about eighty, I'll think about it."

As I have talked to people over the years about the monastic lifestyle, I have been asked a great many questions. At first the more superficial questions often crowd out the basic ones. In fact, I've noticed that people ask three kinds or levels of questions. The questions that usually come most readily refer to the outward appearance of the lifestyle. These questions often reflect a stereotype of monks and nuns, which I myself had before I really came to know any people in the religious life. The media and literature often exacerbate the mystique of the lifestyle. A child once asked me very seriously, "You can't really fly, can you?" People are invariably curious about the strange nature of the traditional habit that I wear, why I have knots in my rope belt, and why I call it a cincture, or girdle. (The two large knots at the ends serve only for puppies to chew on or to be caught in wheelchairs, but the three small knots were tied at my first profession and symbolize the three-fold vow of poverty, chastity, and obedience.) People want to know why nuns wear a veil, or why sisters in my community for the most part no longer wear one. I am often asked why we call our dining rooms "refectories" and our regular times in chapel "the office." I have been asked why monastics call the rooms we sleep in "cells." (Actually the term was used in monasteries to denote a contemplative space long before it was used in prisons!) These are all good questions, but they don't go beneath the surface appearance of the life.

The second kind of questions has to do with practi-calities, such as: "What do you do all day?" and "How do you support yourselves?" These, too, are valid questions, and I will discuss them later. But there is a third level of questions that most people I have spoken to never seem to get around to asking, though they are fundamental and were the first that came to me when I was faced with my own call: "Why are there monks and nuns *any-way*? What purpose do they serve, what on earth—or in heaven—are they *for*?" That is where I always choose to start a discussion on the religious life.

What is its purpose? Christians believe that the pur-pose and end of all individuals and organizations is to give glory to God. Saint Irenaeus, the second-century Bishop of Lyons, wrote: "The glory of God is a human being fully alive." Applying Irenaeus's insight to human organizations, we might paraphrase: "The glory of God is a human community fully alive." Are Anglican com-munities that espouse the religious life today fully alive? Are we striving toward that end? And what distinguishes religious communities from other societies dedicated to the glory of God and service to God's creation? Do we have a particular function in the body of Christ? I believe that we do, but we need to reexamine continually the *radical purpose* of monasticism, in order to try to articulate its perennial and contemporary nature. Unfortunately, the religious life is most generally known by its surface aspects, and to some extent its outdated and unhelpful trappings. The lifestyle is too often either romanticized or vilified. It is always necessary to look anew at what is essential to the purpose and what is extraneous. My community, for example, discerned at one time that we would keep the traditional long habit to be worn on appropriate times and places as a viable liturgical garment. The habit has symbolic value. The main garment, the tunic, is fashioned in the shape of a *tau* cross. The rope belt can symbolize commitment, and at the ceremony of first profession three small knots are added, symbolizing the vow of poverty, chastity, and obedience. The scapular, which is an extra piece worn over the shoulders, symbolizes service. The head piece, or veil, however, which of course men religious don't wear, symbolizes outdated notions of the impropriety of women showing their hair, and so we almost always wear the traditional habit without the veil.

On the other hand, experimentation needs to be just that, and therefore open to reversal. In the 1970s we wondered if the Great Silence—a time of quiet that most monastics keep from evening to after the early morning prayers—was also an outdated concept. After a week of dispensing the silence, we hurriedly put it back; for one reason, we found it was much more likely that we would not bite each other's heads off if we had a little quiet before the workday began. We recognized that silence was an integral part of our life together and apart.

It is particularities of the lifestyle such as these that a person interested in joining a community often asks about. The religious life embraces both the more easily noticed aspects and more basic ones. A lifestyle, in order to serve its purpose, must indeed *serve* its *purpose.* That is to say, a particular way of living should be a fitting context for the life to be lived. The lifestyle of a merchant seaman or a sales representative must accommodate much travel and long absences from home; the life of an academic must include time for research and writing, and must plan for vacations in the summer; the lifestyle of many farmers is still shaped by the seasons, and so on. The lifestyle of a religious community, in order to fulfill its role in the body of the church and in the larger community, needs several components. Silence is an important one of them. A daily rhythm is another, and the times in chapel reciting the daily office provide that. A room to oneself—personal space to think and process, to study, pray, and journal—is another. The common meal and shared time for decision-making and discussion are others.

Each lifestyle has both a practical component (like timeframes and pace) and a less concrete component: the manner in which it is lived. As an example, there are different time schedules for a sales representative and a monk, and there is also quite a different pace and rhythm to changing planes at airports, as compared to going regularly into chapel for prayer. The lifestyle of Western monasticism has its distinctive atmosphere or milieu, including such aspects as a call to radical discipleship; the commitment of the life under vow; relationships and leadership in celibate community; and monastic prayer and ministry. Someone once asked me what were the most basic elements of the religious life.

I found myself replying, "Celibacy, coenobium, and psalmody," or in more modern language, but still alliteratively, "Chastity, community, and chant." Those elements are part of what we religious do all day.

As an English literature major in college I had come across John Donne's great sermon containing the words "No man is an island." Believe it or not this was a revelation to me, because I had always felt very individual and removed from others. Another person's death knell tolls for *me*? What could that mean? And then I came to know about what the meteorologists call the Butterfly Effect: the idea that if a butterfly chances to flap his wings in Beijing in March, then by August hurricane patterns in the Atlantic will be completely different. This in turn helped me understand better Paul of Tarsus's metaphor of the newly forming community of the early church as a single organism, a body, made up of many parts or members. Seeing the human body as an image of the human community woke me to a whole new way of seeing relationship: Christ being the head, and each member of the body having its distinct and proper function. Therefore all members are necessary to the body's health, and all are to be honored in order for the body to be "fully alive." Everything I choose and do for good contributes to the body's health; every unthinking or selfish thing affects it adversely. As Paul wrote, "If one member suffers, all suffer together with it; if one member is honored, all rejoice together with it" (1 Corinthians 12:26).

When I was stationed in our convent in Augusta, Georgia, in the 1970s, I heard an address during a Quiet Day at the convent that impressed me profoundly. In speaking of Paul's metaphor of the body of Christ, the speaker said that those who enter the religious life are the *eyes* of the body. I have wondered about this for many years. The eyes are not the most vital of the body's organs—not as vital, for instance, as the heart or the pancreas—but their function is, nevertheless, of prime importance. Eyes represent vision, clarity, and prophecy. Both our outer and our inner eyes record images of what has been seen, and from these phenomena form new images of future probabilities and desired ends.

Of course, qualities of insight and vision belong to every member of the human race, and, in varying degrees, to all human institutions. We may ask: What makes these qualities particularly descriptive of the religious life? What does it mean to seek to see the truth, the reality of things?

In the first place, for the eye to see accurately, there must be a vantage point from which to see, a place of perspective. As was said above, a "wilderness" often affords such a space. There needs to be some distance from the eye to the object upon which it is focused. If I stand twelve inches from a Van Gogh painting, all I see are vibrant brushstrokes; I need to back up across the room in order to see the structure and content of the painting. In terms of inner perception, such a backing up, or backing off, implies a mental perspective—both on my own inner agenda, and on the demands of external circumstances. If all I can see are images of my own clamorous desires, amid the constant daily bombardment of visual and tactile stimuli, I am incapable of taking in a larger picture. I cannot get past the brushstrokes. We need quality space and time to process raw experience into meaning.

There is a recurrent human need not only to back up across the room, but to find uncluttered space and time away from our daily routine—on a trout stream, a mountain, or a desert, or perhaps in the guest facilities of a monastic community. Like my little room in the West Village, the physical space may not be large, but there does need to be quiet and some freedom from distraction. We need space to listen to ourselves and contemplate. "What is really going on for me? What am I feeling about it? What do I want to do with it?" This is the purpose of a retreat—backing away from an overload of data, in order to *advance* into focus and clarity.

Secondly, in order to see clearly we also need the desire to see what really *is* and not what *should be,* not what would be easier or more pleasant to see. People who are able to see what really *is* include children before they go to school, artists, scientists, and contemplatives. These persons tend to approach and see reality with an attitude of openness and awe. I once asked a quantum physicist whether the people in his profession ever used the word *wonder,* and he said: "Oh, yes!" A child is conventionally taught in school to paint the sky blue. Before that, the child may paint the sky any color. Is the sky really blue at this moment, or is it gray or yellow or lavender or pink or white? (El Greco once saw and painted the sky over Toledo as green.) Is that person with white hair really old? Is that policeman really a bully? Is that person who is smiling at me really happy? Is that widow really sorrowing, or does she feel an overwhelming relief? The seeker of truth asks these questions and does not stop at conventional expectations and social stereotypes.

In the third place, because a given vision may differ from the common norm, seeing what really *is* constitutes a challenge. To open our eyes to the multidimensional reality of a thing is partly a gift and partly an arduously acquired discipline. The person who sees clearly must have a talent for reality. In addition, there must be the moral discipline to practice, and the courage to exercise this gift. The reason for discipline and courage is that seeing the truth, and then speaking it, is often unpopular and even risky. Does the emperor really have those new clothes on—and, further, is it my call to shout out that I don't see them? Small children can get away with speaking the truth, but sooner or later the grown-ups warn them to keep what they see to themselves.

The one who sees clearly must seek for the wisdom to know whether to speak out of that knowledge. It is never enough just to be right. The more important thing is to be loving. It may or may not be the loving thing to tell a destitute person that they have no proper clothes on. It might be loving to speak that truth if you were offering the person your coat or some shoes. But speaking the truth in love does not necessarily mean you will be thanked for it.

If seeing and speaking the truth—both in its glorious and dreadful aspects and all the nuances in between—is so risky, why have so many people throughout the ages felt called to pursue that way? I believe that the answer to that question is freedom, and the peace that accompanies spiritual freedom, though it may well pass our understanding. Jesus promised that the truth would make us free. There is no freedom without truth, despite the pain that often accompanies the process.

Throughout human history there have been individuals who, despite the risk of suffering, have been called to see and then speak out and act beyond safe positions and socially acceptable norms. Many such persons fled to the deserts or mountains to obtain a perspective—both an inner and outer vista—from which to see more clearly. Some eventually came together and formed communities. After the death of the Roman emperor Decius in 251, the persecutions of Christians diminished to the extent that small house church communities were able to survive the remaining persecutions, and by the early fourth century the Christian church had become a dominant force in society. As Christianity spread, there emerged an image of the holy ascetic, the one who fled to the desert—predominantly the unpopulated regions of Egypt west of the Nile—to seek a life of austerity and contemplation. Contemplation can be described as "quiet regard." It can just as readily be an exercise in strenuously confronting inner conflict. In the case of many of the early desert monastics, contemplation was anything but a restful and quiet exercise. It was thought by some that as the church became established in the cities, the demons retreated to the deserts! This was certainly reported to be the case with the most renowned of the early hermits, Saint Anthony the Great of Egypt. A year after Anthony died, Saint Athanasius, who was Anthony's close friend, wrote his *Life of Anthony* describing the hermit's valiant contention with, and subjection of, the demons who assailed him.

Such struggles were common. One of the desert mothers, Amma Syncletia, said:

> In the beginning there are a great many battles and a good deal of suffering for those who are advancing towards God and afterwards, ineffable joy. It is like those who wish to light a fire; at first they are choked by the smoke and cry, and by this means obtain what they seek. . . . So we also must kindle the divine fire in ourselves through tears and hard work.[1]

As we read of the struggles and austerities of the desert, they may seem not so very far removed from our own modern struggles with the "demons" of addictions and neuroses. Men and women then, as now, needed human help as well as divine grace in discerning and healing the malfunctions of body, mind, and spirit. Certainly the desert fathers and mothers had a steady stream of disciples who sought them out in the wild places to ask for "a word." People who became aware of their own psychic and spiritual wounds sought guidance and clarity from those who had survived and gained wisdom from similar inner struggles. Perhaps it is not too fanciful to suggest that the modern "deserts" to which we in the West flee to receive help and healing as we encounter our demons are the offices of psychotherapists, the meetings of Twelve Step programs, and the conference rooms of monasteries and convents.

Even in the earliest desert tradition we find, in conjunction with the desire for the silence and solitude needed to do the soul's inner work, a deep-seated love of the neighboring brothers and sisters, and of the disciples who came for guidance. Many men and women felt the need for the stability and support of a likeminded society. Saint Pachomius, a soldier before his conversion in 313, is reported to have been the first to address this need in any significant way. He founded a monastery in Egypt to which he brought his experience of army discipline; its rule was hierarchical and severe. Yet Pachomius also made provisions for leniency. Respecting both the eremitical (solitary) and coenobitical (community) life, he drew up a rule that made things easier for the less proficient, but did not check the asceticism of the more spiritually experienced. He realized that those of his brothers who were acquainted only with the eremitical life might become discouraged if the everyday cares of community life were forced on them too abruptly. He therefore allowed them to devote their whole time to spiritual exercises, himself taking on all the burdensome work of the daily chores. What a refreshing idea! If we translate that to our own times, we can imagine the Superior, or the leadership of the community, washing the dishes and cleaning the bathrooms so that the novices might devote themselves entirely to spiritual reading and prayer!

To this day we have both the individual seer who lives apart as well as those who create around themselves a sanga, an ashram, a number of disciples, or a group of like-minded peers who form a community. These groupings are social organisms designed to give support and context to a particular call to seek and serve God. As a religious order grows, of course, not everyone who is attracted and comes to share the life will be called to be a truth-seeker in the same way. Not everyone is called to be an elder, prophet, or spiritual guide. Saint Teresa of Avila, a great mystic and contemplative herself, wrote:

> So it does not follow that, because all of us in this house practice prayer, we are all perforce to be contemplatives. That is impossible; and those of us who are not would be greatly discouraged if we did not grasp the truth that contemplation is something given by God, and, as it is not necessary for salvation and God does not ask it of us before He gives us our reward, we must not suppose that anyone else will require it of us.[2]

I have sometimes found that the hardest thing for me in community is respecting another sister who does not seem to me to be choosing the "road less traveled," the

14

narrow way, as I understand it. I do always try to remind myself that what may seem apparent to me about the way of another is, in fact only *apparent,* and that the way I choose to live is only what *I* am called to live. Period. Divine reality transcends appearances, and is a much more loving, complex, and beautiful way of seeing. There are as many ways to seek truth as there are human beings.

I try to remember that to be called to a particular way of prayer or a particular lifestyle does not mean to be *preferred;* to be chosen does not mean to be part of an elite. What is given to each person will be what is required of them. The call and gift of truth-seeking and truth-speaking is a capacity within each human being. It is further manifested in certain individuals, as Teresa notes in the citation above, in a way that marks them out and sets them apart. These persons understand the way of truth-seeking as their primary way of being in the world. It does not make them better than other people, anymore than a person with 20/20 eyesight is a *better* person than one with a cataract. Inner vision is simply a gift among a myriad others to be used and practiced.

I remember that when I was twelve years old, about eight members of my extended family were gathered one summer out on the screened porch at my grandfather's place in the country. We were playing a game: the point was to go around the group and ask each person "Who are you?" Most of us gave the usual answers— what we did, where we lived—but when my turn came I replied: "I am a student of the truth." I do not remember if this surprised the grown-ups or not, because my overwhelming reaction was my surprise at myself! I had never before identified myself in that way.

The way of the truth-seeker is not a *better* way, and it may be said to be atypical. The monastic follows a particular calling that bears witness to the primacy of the holy. The monastic, though set apart, is not really marginal to society; it has been suggested that the nun or monk as archetype is central to a society's deepest yearnings and hopes. In times of stress or disaster an individual or society may turn to its seers, prophets, or monastics for hope and spiritual guidance. The truly destitute and marginalized generally have a sense that they are at the fringes of society, but the monastic properly feels centered in the very heart of humanity and reality.

The human being is inextricably a being and a doer, a contemplator and an actor. What is the good of seeing a situation clearly and not acting upon that knowledge? Contrary to the common stereotypes of the contemplative as "self-absorbed," "fuzzy-headed," "absent-minded," or "in the clouds," I have found that contemplation invariably renders me not less efficient, but more. When I have time and space to contemplate a situation, I can much more quickly move through discernment and prioritization to decision and action. Around other people, even a moment's worth of contemplation allows me to respond with care rather than react instinctively. If a thing is important, it is worth "sleeping on"; and such contemplative space usually pays off.

It can be alarming to wake up to ourselves. A human being "sticks out" of nature; the word "exist" comes from Greek and Latin roots meaning "to stand out." Our very existence has that quality of standing apart, of perspective, which we mentioned above as necessary to clear vision and self-awareness. I remember the first time I became aware of this faculty. I was sleeping over at a little friend's house—we must have been about seven or eight years old. We were in her bedroom and I was sitting on a pink chenille bedspread—the kind with little cotton tufts on it. I became aware of myself noticing a certain little tuft, and then became aware of myself being aware of it. And being aware of being aware of being aware. That realization was both scary and very exciting. We human beings are capable, in some way, of seeing ourselves; not as others see us, and certainly not as God sees us, but ever more realistically as we persevere in truth-seeking.

But before we draw nearer to a realistic understanding of ourselves, many of us tend to perceive ourselves in terms of dualities, of mirror images. We see ourselves as the perfectionist and the klutz, the princess and the pauper, Spiderman and the troubled teenager, genius and idiot, hulk and weakling, holy saint and criminal, tyrant and victim, and so on. I saw myself at one time as a needy little orphan waif and as the aloof and self-sufficient Queen of Sheba! Recognizing these images may be the necessary first step to self-knowledge. The danger comes when we think of ourselves as either better, stronger, or holier than we really are—*or* more helpless or worthless. All perceptions of ourselves fall short of the truth. Sometimes our self-images are benign, and often they are creative tools in the process of self-knowledge, but to identify ourselves with one or more of these images completely is to consent to living a lie.

Only God can discern how much we are able to see and choose clearly. Wisdom is both a gift and a discipline. At any moment, or any stage in my life, I may not be given the gift of clear sight; I may have—so to speak—inner cataracts or retinal damage that are not my fault, but which I have acquired through nature or nurture or simple immaturity. On the other hand, I may, for selfish reasons, choose on some level not to see and stand for the truth. Luckily I am told to try to see, but not to *judge* in myself or in others which is the case. That is God's job.

The difficulty of seeing and embracing truth is a compelling reason why the religious life is such a hard one. It is comforting to know that we are not asked by God or anyone else to succeed but only to persevere, and to trust we will be given grace for the inner journey. Its purpose is to seek, see, speak, and then serve out of a passion for the divine reality whose word is life and who says to us, "Come and see."

CHAPTER TWO

Hearing the Call

What is a "call"? At home in the convent a sister will say my name, and if I hear it, she has gotten my attention. Occasionally, when I have a lot of things on my mind, I don't hear my name called. If it is, say, late in the evening and I'm tired, I am very tempted to *pretend* that I haven't heard. In any case, if my sister thinks the matter important, she will call me again. When she finally gets my attention, how do I respond? Hopefully I turn to her with a welcoming smile; sometimes, I am sorry to say, I have responded with a furrowed brow, a minimum of politeness, and barely disguised impatience.

The word "call" has a technical meaning in the religious life that is not so different from everyday usage. I think God called me many times before I heard—and then, when I did, it was very easy to pretend I hadn't. Or hadn't heard clearly and specifically. And then, when I could no longer pretend that I hadn't heard, I did not at first respond with a welcoming smile!

At the age of thirty-four I was living in a tiny apartment in Greenwich Village, about six years after I had been baptized in a very "high" Anglo-Catholic church in London. Back in this country, however, I had put my doctoral work on hold in order to follow what I thought was a "call" to write plays. I was studying acting and playwriting in the Village, and going to the local Episcopal church. I kept in touch with my priest-mentor in England, Father Langton, who had baptized me and whose great goodness and loving wisdom had made a profound impression on me. It was he who had prepared the ground for me finally to admit the inconvenient truth that the two greatest longings of my life came together in the person of Jesus. From a very early age I had seen myself as a truth-seeker, and Jesus is recorded as having said, "I am the truth." And I had been searching for a "significant other" who could understand me and not be put off by that search for truth.

In the past I too often had spoken my truth in a manner that was strident, unrelenting, and sometimes abrasive. This put off the young men I talked to, who soon avoided any real conversation, and seemed primarily intent on getting me into bed. I was unhappy that the men I went out with, after the first few meetings, invariably wanted to move into my space—physically and emotionally. It felt crowded. Having my own space— that little room, kitchenette, and bath—to myself seemed very important to me at the time. On the other hand, the felt presence of Jesus' spirit had the opposite effect. That presence seemed totally unintrusive, and, in fact, made my space "our" space in a way that made me feel peaceful and happy. Although I could not have articulated it then, I fell in love with God.

About that time I wrote to Father Langton in England about, among other things, the need to be by myself, on my own. I told him that I supposed that after I had written "The Great American Poetic Drama" I would probably end up living like a nun. I meant the line as a sort of humorous throwaway. In his reply, Father Langton mentioned casually that he knew that sometimes finishing one's education was good reason for putting off exploring a call to become a nun, but he did not know if writing plays was.

I then went into a sort of psychic power failure. Me, a nun? Seriously? No way! After three days of repressing the whole thing, I wrote down all the reasons that I could not possibly become a nun. The only ones that I can remember today are that I would have to give up plucking between my eyebrows, and that I would never again own and drive a little black MG sports car with red leather upholstery. I was all set to "kick against the goads," as Saint Paul did, until they stopped kicking back. Eventually, however, I was dazzled by the truth and had to stop kicking. After more correspondence with my holy mentor, a good deal more prayer and some tears, I moved through and beyond my anxieties.

Months passed. No doubt I should have visited a number of religious communities, as most people who are inquiring about the religious life today are urged to do, but I didn't. I finally looked through a little booklet I found in my parish church that had a page each about the various monastic orders in the Episcopal Church. (Nowadays you can go straight to the Internet!) At first I was attracted to a teaching order that ran two schools and supported their sisters in continuing their education. I thought: "Well, I could do this crazy nun thing and finish my PhD and be a scholar after all. Have my cake and eat it too!" There was one problem, however: one of the communities in the booklet was a very small group on Long Island, who stayed home and prayed to God and interceded for the world. Every time I passed that page the tears began to come. I think my tears were mostly of self-pity—I really didn't want to do *that!* But after some more feet-dragging and goad-kicking, I finally applied to try my vocation there as an enclosed contemplative Franciscan nun.

Every call to the religious life is a radical call; of course the further the lifestyle diverges from that of the prevailing culture, the more radical it *seems.* But taken in its literal sense, to be radical does not mean to be "far out," but to be rooted or "root-like," to be the basis and support of something else. In that sense, a call to monasticism is a call to live the tap-root of Christianity: to love God with all one's strength, mind, heart, and soul, and to love one's neighbor. But for many people, perhaps most people, the call does seem to cross the line from different to weird. I remember sitting in a diner on Lexington Avenue with my brother—my only sibling, to whom I have always been very close—having a good-bye cup of coffee before I went to become an enclosed nun. My brother was upset. He said "Honey, you are doing a crazy thing, and what really bothers me is that you don't have the symptoms of a crazy person."

For some people, the call and their response *appear* to be simultaneous. I know a sister who was walking down the street and saw two nuns walking toward her, and knew then and there that she was "called." Yet no doubt the sister who saw the two nuns on the street also had some unconscious awareness of her deepest desire before the moment of truth came to her. With most people it takes longer, and many become aware of their call long before they are able to respond. I have talked to a number of women and men who say they felt a call to be a monk or nun when they were in their teens and twenties, and then put it "on hold" while they took up careers, raised families, or became parish priests, until their lives once again became free of responsibilities and they were able to go ahead. This capacity for a delayed response is now true for divorced people as well: since the new canons on remarriage in the church were passed by the General Convention of the Episcopal Church a few decades ago, a person who has been divorced may have a bishop confirm that the former marriage is indeed terminated in the eyes of the church, and such a person may be remarried in the church. That makes it also possible for religious communities in the Episcopal Church to accept divorced men and women who have had their marital status so regularized by a bishop. The marriage vow has, of course, to be annulled before the celibate vow can be taken.

Whether conscious or semiconscious, whether immediate or protracted, every call and life choice has *some* history. Before my own moment of epiphany when I received the letter from my mentor, I see now that I had been on a long journey into truth, into trust, and into Christ. From childhood I always felt an attraction to what I later came to define as spiritual freedom. Here is an example: I was very attracted to the freedom of being equally at ease with men and women. In this I had been extremely lucky. I had been sent as a child to a very progressive elementary school in New York City under the aegis of Teachers College at Columbia University, where, beginning in the first grade, the boys and girls were treated equally. Boys could and did take cooking, and girls took carpentry, and so on. When as an adult I heard that in Christ "there is no longer male and female" (Galatians 3:28) it resonated with my earliest experience. I have at times felt unjustly treated by a male-dominated culture, but because of my early experience I have never personally felt inferior to any man.

Once I had heard my call and felt it to be my deepest desire and my soul's freedom, I had to find the grace and the courage to act upon it. This grace and courage, too, had a precedent in my life. When I was in graduate school at Stanford University, I had an experience that I now see had a profound effect on my ability to choose and to find the courage to act upon what I felt as my deepest desire. I was working toward an MA in creative writing. At that time, in the 1950s, there was a select seminar in poetry writing taught by the poet and critic Yvor Winters. This seminar consisted of a small number of graduate students and met in Winters's office. Most of the students were men; there was one other woman besides me. The men were all very talented, confident, and, as I remember, tall. Winters and one of the other men smoked pipes, one smoked cigars. After we had done our work, Winters would say something like, "The ladies may be excused." I supposed that the men sat and smoked and talked after we left. I had no idea what they talked about, but I very much wanted to be an integral member of that select group and not a mere appendage. At that time I was dating a young man who was a graduate student in the history department. He smoked a pipe. So I asked him to teach me how. The next time the poetry seminar met, I quietly got out my pipe, filled it expertly from my tobacco pouch, tamped it down with my (borrowed) pipe tool and lit it easily with my (borrowed) pipe lighter. The conversation had stopped and all eyes were on me. Then professor Winters said, "Hand me your pipe." Since he was smiling one of his rare smiles, I did. He dumped out the tobacco I had so carefully put in and said, "You don't want to smoke that terrible aromatic stuff. Here, have some of my Old Mariner." He refilled my pipe, lit it, and handed it back to me. That day and thereafter the "ladies" were not excused, but stayed on until the meeting was over.

A call to a prophetic and radical role in the body of Christ is always a call to human freedom and equality. In the very beginning, religious community was a place where men and women could exercise an equal kind of authority. In the Middle Ages some men and women were called to the great double monasteries such as the one at Whitby, governed by the Abbess Hilda. The twelfth-century Hildegard of Bingen is a prime example of a woman religious who gave spiritual direction and counsel to men as well as women, including abbots, priests, bishops, and even to the Holy Roman Emperor. Even in later centuries when the male hierarchy was in ascendance, many strong-spirited women saw the religious life as an alternative to marriage, where their gifts of creativity and leadership might be most richly and freely employed.

I am focusing primarily on the call to life in community, but because we are all called to grow in love for our neighbors, what pertains to life in community also applies in some part to hermits and solitaries. It has been said that to be a healthy hermit one should have lived in religious community for twenty years before asking to live as a solitary. Whether or not this is applicable in all cases, the statement bears some truth. The solitary life is best lived by a person who has matured psychologically and spiritually, and life in community is a prime context in which to grow in those ways. The life of a hermit should not be an escape from the difficulties of living or the responsibilities of relationship. It should be a tested and affirmed choice. An example of such a choice happened in our order. One sister felt a call to live as a solitary after decades of life in community, and, together with a discernment committee of three of her sisters, explored how she might test that vocation. She did live as a hermit for two different periods, one in a hermitage on the grounds of a Roman Catholic order, and one in a cabin in the woods, before she chose to live out the contemplative aspect of her vocation within her original community by lengthening her times of prayer and quiet.

In fact, most hermits are not entirely solitary; they have persons and communities by whom they are supported and others to whom they are accountable. They also have some ministry, whether spiritual direction, intercession, writing, or art, by which they, in turn, interact with or contribute to the body of Christ, of which we are all made members at our baptisms. Again, "No man is an island" (although my brother once remarked that he sometimes feels like a very long peninsula!) and no man or woman, even if they live alone, is isolated from the body of Christ or our common humanity.

Another aspect of the call is that it may be heard at first in a diffuse manner that does not specify the final choice of lifestyle. A young man or woman, for instance, might identify a call to "love God and help people," and interpret that as joining the Peace Corps, teaching, working for Habitat for Humanity, or going to medical school or seminary, and only later feel the call refocused as "go to the monastery or convent." This more specific call generally makes itself known by the idea appearing in one's thoughts repeatedly and over a period of time.

Since the religious life is countercultural, the call most often manifests itself as a call to leave, or witness against, the prevalent values of society: the power of a few at the expense of many; acquisition and consumerism at the expense of the poor and of the earth; and sexual license at the expense of human dignity. The monastic is never called to hate the earth itself or its inhabitants, but only those forces that diminish or degrade God's creation.

In the very beginning of the monastic life in the West, men and women were called to a life that would stand against the corruptions and excesses of the Roman Empire and court society. There were, for the Christian community, three major reasons to flee that prevailing culture. The first was distress at the practices of slavery and forced labor, and the extremely wide gap between the affluent "haves" and the oppressed "have-nots." Second was disgust with the rampant sexual license and the unbridled eroticism of the imperial court. And a third reason was an abhorrence of political corruption—the self-serving, cruel, and often whimsical power wielded by many of the emperors and their minions. It may be fanciful, but thought-provoking, to suggest that these three reactions to imperial Rome that prompted the flight to the desert might be the seminal bases for the three aspects of the monastic vow: voluntary poverty, chastity, and obedience.

In a society where forces for self-interest and exploitation *prevail,* the prophetic stance against them is, by definition, unpopular. Further, a stance against social norms tends not only to be unpopular, but threatening to the majority. Often, like Jesus, modern prophets are killed: "Therefore I send you prophets, sages, and scribes, some of whom you will kill and crucify, and some you will flog in your synagogues and pursue from town to town" (Matthew 23:34). Sometimes inconvenient prophetic witness is trivialized and sentimentalized: how many representations have you seen of Saint Francis with the excruciating stigmata as opposed to the saint of songbirds and rabbits? The monastic way of radical self-gift is not better or more perfect than other vocations, but it is rarer. Sometimes what is rare is prized; sometimes it seems alien, and raises suspicion and fear. There is a reason why there is a road less traveled, and a narrow way that only a few find. Suspicion of the unusual, when it applies to religious vocation, may prompt discouraging remarks by relatives or even pastoral mentors to those inquiring about the call, such as: "Why would a young person like you, of such advantages or personal attractiveness, want to throw yourself away in a life like that?" Why indeed? This is the great question, and has perhaps no fully rational answer. Once, when we were still youngsters, my brother said to me, "You are a 'why' person and I am a 'how' person." As it turned out, I am a Christian nun and he is an atheist and a scientist. God knows why.

It is important to remember that a call is an invitation, and not a command. Any invitation, of course, can remain unanswered, put "on hold," or not responded to. Even if the person called feels a compelling urgency to change his or her lifestyle in a radical way, there is in any healthy situation a choice to be made. Luke's story of the rich ruler is a poignant example: "When Jesus heard this, he said to him, 'There is still one thing lacking. Sell all that you own and distribute the money to the poor, and you will have treasure in heaven; then come, follow me.' But when he heard this, he became sad; for he was very rich" (Luke 18:22–23). As far as we know, Jesus did not urge him any further. The call to radical discipleship must be responded to and chosen *freely.* We are made in the image of God: that is, we are creatures called to love and to choose.

Yet, in a sense, though the choice is free, it may not always be experienced that way. My own call may be said to have begun as a sense that I needed to "seek and follow the truth, no matter what the cost." The name that came to me for that was "the inner way." Part of that early experience was a strong sense of urgency. Even though I knew that I *might* resist the call and take an easier way, I felt somehow that my "yes" was inevitable if I were not to betray my truest nature.

A very vivid example of resisting my call to be a truth-seeker comes to mind. I was in London, in my early twenties, staying with a friend from college while I looked for a place of my own. My life was in a mess— I was depressed and could not see where I was going, or wanted to go. I had this vague sense that I was called to be and do something worthwhile, and that it probably had to do with writing, but I felt no support from family or friends except for this one friend. At the time I was dating an Englishman who wanted to marry me but whom I did not love. The possibility of giving up, of choosing the mediocre over the good, was for me at that time "stopping all this soul-searching and struggle and marrying the Englishman and having lots of little blond English children." Such a course was very tempting, but dimly I knew it would be like hanging up the phone on my true call. My friend from college, a wise and perceptive young woman, also sensed this and became extremely tired of my depression and lack of purpose, my slovenliness in her house, and, in a real sense, my betrayal of our friendship. One morning—I'll never forget it—she was in the kitchen slicing tomatoes on the wooden drain board, and she said to me: "If you don't pull yourself together and find a place to live on your own *today*, I'm going to ask you to leave, and I never want to see you again." Those were the cruelest and the kindest words I had ever heard. I cried, picked myself up, found a room of my own, and moved into it that week. With help from my friend and grace from God, the urgency of my call to my particular path was reawakened. The path into the unknown seemed again possible and desirable. My life and my spirits started upward from that point.

"No matter what the cost" is a phrase that underlines the radical and the difficult nature of the call to discipleship. It is a way of emptying, but there are two kinds of emptying. One is chosen, and one is imposed. When your house burns down and you are stripped of all your possessions, that is not a good kind of emptying! When you freely choose to give your warm winter coat to someone who needs it more than you, that is a very different thing. This opportunity for choice is also true in the realm of psyche and spirit. Often it has not been easy for me to discern between what is a holy divesting of my ego/self, and a not-so-holy conciliation or "cop out." The difference lies between the gift of true surrender and the false gesture of submission in the face of a misconceived demand. We cannot freely give what we do not have.

Choice is an important matter in the discerning of a call. There is a great difference between self-gift that is solidly based on trust in God, and unconsidered and self-willed recklessness. Extreme or radical self-gift is only healthy—and may only be possible—when there is confidence that the call is from a loving God, and not from a tyrant god or a trickster god or one's own super-ego.

If the call is from a lover to the beloved, it presumes an exchange of mutual gift. In my own case the Divine Lover did not compel me, but wooed me to give up my limited ownership of self so that I might receive the bounty of spiritual freedom.

Trust in God is hard, and won slowly—risk by risk, life experience by life experience. I knew a monk who had an extremely untrustworthy and erratic infancy and childhood, and whose capacity for trust was damaged so cruelly and so early that he could never grow to trust his brothers and superiors in community. The emotions of his parents had been erratic, and family rules seemed to change overnight. Yet not to obey those inconsistent and therefore unobeyable "rules" meant he did not receive what he needed to survive—including sufficient affirmation and love. Though not nearly as extreme, I had some of the same early experience. Anxiety was like the air I breathed. I remember when I was in my forties, in the midst of intensive psychotherapy, I awoke one morning with a very strange feeling. I realized that what I was feeling was "*not* anxiety"—and so it was the first time that I knew what *anxiety* felt like! Before then, anxiety to me was what water is to a fish.

To trust that God will indeed return to us thirtyfold, sixtyfold, or one-hundredfold is more difficult than trusting that an e-ticket will get us on the plane when we were only used to paper ones. Love cannot be pinned down or guaranteed. Love does not offer certainty. We may never in this life be certain, though by grace we may become confident. A lovely word, "confident"—deriving from the Latin roots *con* and *fido*—literally, "with faith." How hard for so many of us to be confident that there is a God who is just and loving, much less one who is passionately eager to shower us with blessings. Nevertheless, the call of mature love *is* to grow into trust: to move, in God's grace and by our own desire, from confusion and anxiety to integration and peace.

Hearing and answering my call to "the inner way" felt to me like putting my toe in the river, and if the piranha fish didn't eat it off, then trying my foot; then if that was safe, my whole leg, and so on, until, almost a decade after I first perceived a call to radical Christian discipleship, I came to the plunge of total immersion in baptism: the spirit's surrender—a spiritual death and rebirth. The further journey of moving from anxiety to relative inner peace came two decades after that. The journey is never ended. If I listen each day, I may continue to hear echoes of what the prophet Elijah experienced after the thunder and the fire: the "sound of sheer silence," which is the milieu in which I may hear the call of the Divine Lover.

Each human call to deeper trust and surrender is unique; most experience the call as coming from somewhere and someone else, and not as made up in one's own head. What is true of the general call to trust and more mature love is also true specifically of the call to the religious life. It is never like a neon sign in the sky accompanied by thunder. Very often it is simply an idea that creeps seemingly unbidden into one's thoughts, but it does very often seem like something one could not possibly have imagined on one's own.

It is important to remember that a call to radical discipleship is not synonymous to a call to the religious life. I was very aware of this when I finally identified a monastic calling in myself. The idea of being a nun did not at that time appeal to me at all. I went to my mentor and asked, "Is the religious life a good thing in itself, and not simply a good choice for *me?*" After a moment of silence, he answered, "Yes. A very good thing." I needed to hear that, because a number of other alternatives seemed much more attractive. I needed to know that this "weird" calling was seen by someone whose judgment I trusted as a good thing to choose; not necessarily a better thing, but a good thing in itself. Talking with persons one trusts is a very important thing to do at this point of vocation in order to receive affirmation of a perceived call. It is always good to question—with others, with one's own heart's deepest desire, and with God in prayer.

Once, when I was entertaining the idea of vocation to a certain community, I was on a Manhattan subway. Sitting opposite me was a young couple who were speaking in Spanish, of which I had only rudimentary knowledge. It was obvious that they were very much in love, and by understanding a few words it came to me that they were talking about finding a place to live when they were married. Suddenly it was as if Jesus was sitting beside me. I found myself silently asking him, "Is *that* community the place we want to live together when I make my commitment to you?" I didn't hear any "answer," but I had the feeling that my question was received, and that at least the response was not a negative one.

A radical commitment, as we have indicated above, is a risky business. A further risk is that aiming high incurs the risk of a greater fall. There is an old saying about this: "The devil never attacks noncombatants." If one is consciously seeking the good, evil must be resisted. There is also an old Latin saying: *Corruptio optimi pessimum,* "The corruption of the best is the worst." And as Shakespeare wrote, "Lilies that fester smell far worse than weeds." In a more perfect world it should not be the case, but if a monk bears false witness, or a friar shoplifts, or a sister out of envy publicly denigrates someone, or a religious superior abuses power by sexual or emotional exploitation, it does seem to "smell far worse" than if another did the same thing. A radical public commitment to the gospel injunction to love and justice enjoins radical public accountability.

There is a further risk of distorting the call to the religious life by creating around it a mystique of other-worldliness. An unworldly or otherworldly mystique is destructive because it is a departure from human truth and healthy human relationships that must be rigorously opposed. I once heard a rather chilling story that awoke me to the harm that such a mystique can do. Soon after the changes of Vatican II, a religious sister whose community had just decided to wear secular clothing found herself in a crowded Manhattan subway. Someone behind her pushed her so that she bumped into the person in front of her. The man she had bumped turned, and in a hostile voice said, "Why don't you watch what you're doing!" The sister realized with a jolt that all the time she had worn the habit, no one had ever spoken to her like that—as to any other "ordinary" human being. For most of the people she met, she had been not a person but a prototype. And over time she herself had begun to see herself as subtly different from ordinary human beings.

Something of the same nature once happened to me in a ladies room at an airport back in the days when we traveled in full habit. There was quite a long waiting line, and I was shocked when a woman near the front of the line said, "Sister, please go ahead of me." I almost replied, as I politely refused her offer, that I was sure my bladder was the same size as hers. That is what I mean by mystique. It can be a great obstacle to growing into one's full humanity.

There is a considerable risk that if we enter the religious life it will make us vulnerable to these stereotypes and projections so that we begin to see ourselves through a similar distorted lens. After about ten years in monastic profession, I thought I had been quite careful about avoiding the temptation to envision myself as other than I really was. I knew I felt equally as comfortable in a habit or in "mufti." However, a deepening of the revelation came to me when I was on vacation with my brother and sister-in-law. We were in a boat, fishing, and I was watching an osprey catch the fish that I wasn't catching. I suddenly knew in the core of my being that I was not only *comfortable* both in choir and on the trout stream, but I was exactly the *same person* on the trout stream sipping a beer in my jeans as I was in chapel in my habit chanting the psalms. It was a great sense of integration, but also a warning as to how insidious the temptation is to see the call as "special" in the sense of being somehow differently human. Temptation is human; Jesus knew temptation, but temptations that lead us away from reality—even in the subtlest ways—must be resisted. The temptation to see the religious life as a way to be "better" or more healed or holier or more secure is an insidious one.

It is also tempting to enter the religious life to "find one's niche." There may be a benign way of understanding the "niche" concept, but the danger is in imagining it will confer some kind of safety or magic shield against life's uncertainties and challenges. It won't. More important, it will not provide us with any more worth or identity than we have already. Ultimately a "niche" is just another illusion, and an illusion is at best a distorted truth, and at worst a lie. A novice once told me that she wanted the Order of Saint Helena to be where she would finally find her "niche." That was an unreal expectation and her desire was not filled; eventually she left the community. Our only true "niche" is God, and knowing ourselves as creatures of God. As the writer of the letter to the Hebrews put it: "For here we have no lasting city, but we are looking for the city that is to come" (13:14). Here we have no lasting "niche." Community can be a context for growth and maturity, but it cannot confer true worth, much less one's core sense of identity.

The call to the religious life is also different from other callings because of its intensity. In a way it is a concentrate of life-areas. In most lifestyles there are decisions to be made in three distinct areas: one's career, one's relationships, and one's faith or philosophy. This threefold way of being in the world has its advantages. One young woman who was inquiring about our order told me that when her partner left her the only way she could cope was that she had a prayer group at her church who listened to and supported her, as well as a job that challenged her and required her attention. Another woman went through a period of spiritual dryness when she stopped going to church and found it almost impossible to pray—but her family was warm and supportive and she loved her job. A third person lost her job and could not find work that had any meaning for her. During this time, worship and particularly involvement in a healing group at her church was very meaningful to her, and she had family members who kept in touch and helped her make contacts that led her to consider and obtain a new occupation.

In the monastic life, however, relationships, work, and worship all come in the same "package." A monastic lives, prays, works, plays, and loves in the same primary context of community, and the choice for one of the life-areas is a choice for all three. This makes for a high degree of intensity. In contradiction to a popular notion that life in religious community is one of greater protection and ease, the life is just as, or even more, stressful than any other. In fact, an image that comes to my mind is that of holding a magnifying glass between the sun's rays and dry grass—the intensifying lens may cause enough heat to produce fire. For this reason it is very important that monastics are attentive to individual and communal psychological well-being as well as physical health. This ability to tolerate intensity well also may be of primary importance in discerning a call to a monastic lifestyle. I have known many people who have tried the religious life and have not found the intensity of it sustainable. Even if they feel a call to prayer and celibacy, they find living on their own in an apartment with a job and a church commitment to be more satisfactory.

It is important to discern as soon as possible whether it is appropriate, after the initial sense of call, to explore further. One of the major areas of discernment of vocation is whether an aspirant to the life has enough psychological strength and maturity for self-giving. I have known people who were immature or did not have a strong sense of themselves, and who hoped that community would supply affirmation and protection. It won't. One reason why many religious communities have stopped using titles such as Father Abbot and Mother Superior for their leaders is that these seem to foster dependence in their members. In some Roman Catholic communities in the past, the overarching power of the leaders and the immaturity of the members led to an infantilization that resulted in a dearth of candidates for future leadership. When the superior died, there was no replacement. A good measure of maturity is an integrated sense of self. If the call is to give oneself in love, there must be at least enough self to give authentically. One must have a life before one can "lose" it; one must have a strong sense of self before one can healthily deny it for a greater good. I have known several women who have been in a vocational process for religious life who, before life profession, have wisely said something like this: "I think I'm beginning to see what religious life is really like, and I think I may have a vocation to it, but I feel that there is some work on myself I need to do first."

Once a call has been heard, it must be tested. Since the call is to a function within the body of Christ, and is not simply a call "of the alone to the Alone," discernment must be communal. Traditionally, a seeker at the beginning stage is called an inquirer. After contact and correspondence, a person first makes a short preliminary visit to the community or communities he or she is interested in. I'll never forget my first visit to the Order of Saint Helena. I was told that since I had already had experience of the religious life in another community, I might visit soon, even though it was deep into Lent and not usually the best time for welcome and conversation. I arrived the week before Easter, which culminates in the great holy days of Maundy Thursday, Good Friday, Holy Saturday, and the Great Vigil of Easter. I was told (it sounded like a warning) that silence would be kept until after the first mass on Easter Sunday. This sounded fine to me—I had had five years filled with lots of silence and prayer. But when Holy Saturday arrived the superior, Sister Alice, beckoned to me and we went down to a cottage on the property and talked and talked and talked for hours! That is the purpose of a preliminary visit; it is a time for the inquirer and the brothers or sisters to ask each other all the questions they can think of.

During my forty years in community I have met with hundreds of people who were at this inquiring stage of their journey. There are several matters that generally arise during such an initial exchange. One of the first things I often find myself saying is that the decision facing an inquirer is *not* a decision for the rest of one's life, but simply a decision to collect more data on a live-in basis, a period that is usually called postulancy or candidacy. Unlike marriage, or moving in with a partner, collecting data by living with a community is relatively free of physical and emotional investment. The entire process of commitment to life in community is gradual and lengthy; it usually lasts an average of five years.

If the preliminary visit or visits bode well for both parties, the ordinary next step is to make a longer visit to one of the order's houses. During that visit of about two weeks, an inquirer meets with all or many of the sisters or brothers residing in the house. In our community she lives in the enclosure (where the sisters live), goes to community house meetings where consensual decisions for daily life are made, and works, prays, and recreates with the sisters. A behavioral interview and psychological testing ordinarily are given to the inquirer at this time. In many ways both parties come to know one another a great deal better. Mutual gathering of information of both a statistical and also an interpersonal nature is what these visits are about.

If what we call "the aspirant visit" is fruitful for both the aspirant and the community, she may apply formally to enter the community. This involves submitting copies of documents such as baptismal and confirmation certificates, school transcripts, letters of recommendation, and background checks. If there are no "red flags" after these are reviewed, and the sisters have consulted among themselves, she is received into the community as a postulant—itself a time for more data gathering. To enter as a postulant does imply that she is sufficiently free of any other responsibilities to continue into the novitiate, but there is still no major commitment made, and either the individual or the community may decide to discontinue the relationship at any point.

Generally speaking, the period of inquiry is brief, unless there are things to be taken care of, such as a credit card debt to be worked off, a house to be sold, or a pet to be found a home. Postulancy is a time when the person is postulating whether this is the right lifestyle for her, and the community is also discerning whether this is a candidate likely to thrive in their particular community. It generally lasts about six months. After this, she is "clothed" by receiving the habit of the order, and becomes a novice for usually two years of study and further education for the religious life.

One of my favorite analogies for incorporation into community is the heart transplant. Will this heart give life to this body? Will this body accept and thrive with this heart? Incorporation means literally entering into the life-giving system of the body. Before going into heart transplant surgery, every possible test is administered and interpreted. After that, only the actual surgery and recovery will confirm that the transplant was a mutually life-conferring operation.

Those who enter the religious life come from very different educational backgrounds. I remember one novitiate class that I co-taught with the novice master of the men's Order of the Holy Cross. Among our novices were a theologian who was writing and publishing scholarly books on the ante-Nicene fathers and a woman who did not yet have a high school diploma. There were many levels of schooling between those extremes. This class worked because it contained some material on monastic spirituality that was new to all participants, but many classes and personal studies need to be tailored to individual needs and interests.

After the novitiate a woman will make her profession of the vow for one year, to be renewed annually by mutual discernment, usually for two to three years. After this time of incorporation—somewhere around five years—she may request life profession. These stages of incorporation are of ancient origin. Though they have varied from time to time and still vary from community to community, they represent a fairly realistic timeframe. It really does take that long for the process of mutual commitment to be sufficient for a commitment for life. The "honeymoon" or courtship idealisms and enthusiasms must fade away, and after that, a period of disillusionment and need for reorientation usually sets in.

I was fairly starry-eyed when I first came to community, and that is not atypical. I wasn't entirely naive. I knew that the sisters would have human foibles just as I did, but I did somehow expect that my sisters would have the same single-minded ardor and intensity that I did. I didn't expect to find *perfect* people, but I didn't expect to find *ordinary* people either! During the honeymoon period my sisters did seem rather extraordinary—more knowledgeable, welcoming, spiritual, and passionate for justice than any I had ever met. But after many months I found that my expectations—and, yes, projections—were both off-target and an irritation to all concerned. The honeymoon was over! I realized my sisters and brothers in religious life were just as ordinary as I was.

There are challenges in the novitiate other than disillusionment, and one is the difficulty of getting to know and relate to many people all at once. Even though Anglican monasteries and convents are relatively small, there may be as many as ten to fifteen people with whom you will live. That is a lot of relationships to begin all at once, and unlike a parish family or an office staff, these are presumably relationships for life. Furthermore, if a community is intending to establish additional houses, you will need to experience what it is like to know and be known in a context and household different from the one where you first started. Another daunting reality is that no matter how well or warmly the community welcomes you as a mature individual, you are still relating to people who will at some point vote on your acceptance.

Discernment continues during the entire period up to life profession; nevertheless, it is always helpful to begin a thoughtful and deliberate evaluation at the earliest stages. These days, many of the men and women who consider the religious life are people of much varied life experience, and they feel they don't have many years to devote to a process that is not going to work out for them. On the other hand, the time spent in exploring community may be very fruitful no matter what the outcome. Many people who have decided not to persevere at one stage or another still cherish the time spent in community as one of the most important of their lives. Very often it has signified a turning point in their spiritual journey. My own community has many such "alumnae" who are now fulfilled in the lives they finally chose—to name only a few, parish priest, college professor, mother and grandmother, businesswoman, bishop, occupational therapist, and social worker.

There are of course some partings of the way that are not mutual, and are very painful. It can work both ways: sometimes women in whom the community has invested much love and hope choose to leave; sometimes the community itself makes the choice because of increasing friction, aggression, or mutual recrimination. It is to avoid such painful partings that the process of discernment should begin as early as possible. However, this vocation is very much a concern of the Holy Spirit, and needs time for the "match" to become clear. Quite often the likeliest looking applicant ends up not being a good fit for the community, while someone with more questionable educational, emotional, or occupational "credentials" perseveres and grows into a fulfilled and fruitful member. It is hard to invest so much love and concern in someone who eventually departs, but it may well be an important ministry of the religious life to offer such a time and space for life discernment.

As early as the first visit, important issues of motivation should surface. Why does the inquirer want to try this lifestyle? Why now? What does he or she expect to give to it, and receive from it? In my experience, motives have almost always been mixed. There are, of course, the "noble" components of the call—"To know, love, and serve God and God's people." It is not contradictory, but rather complementary, that there may also be more self-serving reasons. Often tucked among the more acceptable motivations one finds a need for security, doubts about sexual identity, a rebound from an unhappy relationship, or even rebellion against family expectations. I knew one postulant whose personality was made up of diverse self-images and who was haunted by her "evil" self. She felt that if she became a nun she would *have* to be good, and that convent life would somehow automatically override her badness, so that instead of judging her, God would love her. This of course was very muddled thinking and bad theology. In the first place God loves us whatever and wherever we are, and in the second, no external force can make us good. Fortunately, God can take *all* of our motives— good, bad, muddled, genuine—and transfigure them all into a solid vocation, either to the religious life or some other commitment. The only real danger lies in repressing or lying about our motives, either to ourselves or to others, as we become aware of them. The call for each person is primarily to deeper self-truth, and to the compassion and love that can only spring from the ground of truth. We are called to bring our full selves—good and less good—to the exploration.

Why is incorporation such a lengthy process? Christianity itself has never been easily grasped; it has a broad scope of practice and mystical depths. At its beginnings, all seekers and initiates went through a lengthy catechumenate before they were fully accepted into the church. As the "eyes of the church," therefore, the religious life needs its own particular catechumenate, which includes experiential knowledge as well as intellectual understanding.

Everyone testing a vocation suffers some form of culture shock. People come from many cultures and social environments, so that some face a geographical adjustment as well as the inevitable monastic culture shock. If you have owned a car and are used to simply getting into it and driving away, it is hard to share it with others or even to remember to sign it out with times of departure and return. It may be somewhat of a shock to find that the local plants exacerbate your allergies, or that the water tastes different, or that the food doesn't agree with you, or that the community's insurance policy limits your choice of a doctor. I used to tell our inquirers that beyond these more immediate things, there are three very usual aspects of postulant culture shock. First, the changes in environment, schedule, and food may result in some physical complaint (my own was gastrointestinal). Second, their prayer life might suffer or "disappear." And third, there will be one sister who makes them feel, "Either she leaves or I leave!" While this transition is taking place, moreover, the postulant is in a vulnerable position. I am told that a lobster, as it ages, must shed its outgrown shell in order to live. In the stages between shells, however, it is very vulnerable and may be eaten by predators. During my novitiate I felt a good deal like that young lobster!

Entering the monastic culture can be difficult both for a young person who does not yet have routine habits and preferences, and for a more mature person who does. As former ways of living are changed and challenged, we can become disoriented and uncertain. Such insecurity may emerge as a kind of territorialism. I have heard that the sign for contentment in Chinese is a woman under her own roof, while the sign for strife is two women under one roof! Sharing a kitchen or any other space with other people can be a real challenge to serenity and sisterly or brotherly love.

Most adults have developed preferences that they feel define them as individuals. When I came to try my vocation as a religious, I knew myself as a person who drove an MG, used *Shalimar* perfume, listened to baroque music, prayed without words kneeling on the floor, wore jeans, had hair down to my waist, and on my little finger wore my father's signet ring, which I had inherited at his death when I was thirteen. To lose all these things that I perceived as part of my identity and to replace them with things that seemed very foreign to me was significant culture shock. Even harder than that was relinquishing a former vocation that I had seen as my core identity. From age twelve to age thirty-four I had seen myself as a writer; if I was not Ellen-the-writer, I did not know who I was. Whether it was ultimately the right thing to do or not, I stopped writing for twenty years. For much of that time I was vulnerable—I did not know who I was, though molecule by molecule I was finding myself as simply an "I am" in the image of the "I AM" of God. Twenty years later, perhaps because my sense of identity was sufficiently weaned from being "a writer," my call to write resurfaced, this time as a gift rather than as a compulsion.

The disorientation of the time of incorporation may be experienced as a dark night of the senses, or of the spirit. One often feels that one cannot return to one's old ways, habits, identifying traits, and values, but one is not yet quite comfortable in the new milieu. A good analogy here is the tadpole, who is in the process of losing tail and gills but whose small lungs and legs are not yet strong enough to breathe the strange new air and leap upon the ground. At this stage for the human "amphibian" there is needed an emotional climate safe enough to support the transition, and some human beings to talk to who have been there before and who can listen and encourage. Accompanying the disorientation may be a deep sense of loneliness and homesickness. Back home, one was in control—one knew where to shop, where the cheapest carwash was, and who was the nearest reliable dentist. Here, one has to ask others for, or be burdened with, a great deal of new information.

The need for help and support applies not only to the imparting of facts. More importantly, support is needed as response to feelings that are aroused in the new person by the disorientation and reorientation of the transition process. It must be strongly emphasized that being responsive to a new person's needs is not a question of seeing the person in transition as a child. The nurture of a child and being available to an adult as a mentor in transition are two entirely different things. It is not altogether surprising that the two in some cases have tended to be confused, either by the new person or by the sisters she talks to, or both; but the tendency must be rigorously resisted. We are called, in mature love, to help bear one another's burdens and to be there for one another.

Even at the early stage of testing vocation two other major issues may surface. The first is that the process of incorporation is *not* a "win or lose" proposition. To many postulants and novices it is tempting to view it as such. All of one's early feelings of parental pressure and expectations may resurface, resulting in a compulsion "to make the grade." In this mindset, to be elected to life profession means to succeed, to "win." Because this attitude is ultimately not a realistic one, monastics who consider that they have "made it" have occasionally been known to leave shortly after profession. They "won," and lo and behold! they did not feel any more secure or worthwhile. It is very tempting to think, "When I am clothed—when I receive the habit—then I will be all right." Then after clothing, one can say to oneself, "Well, when I'm professed it will be all right." But even if a person is elected superior it will not resolve these needs of self-worth or identity. Succeeding, "making it," is not an exercise that leads to fulfillment.

The other common but less-than-helpful concept is seeing the testing of vocation as acceptance or rejection. This area is a little more complex and subtle. The trying of a vocation is not about being accepted as a person. As I have mentioned, a number of our former sisters were and are fully accepted and loved as *persons,* but discernment revealed that community life was not the best lifestyle for them. Incorporation is not about succeeding, nor about acceptance, but about a vocational fit.

These misinterpretations lead to a further misleading concept. It may seem that the data to be gathered during postulancy consists of practical knowledge— which car is parked in the carport and which on the driveway, which times and areas are silent ones, which candles are lit for which class of feast, or which sisters prefer notes in their mailboxes to being approached verbally in the hallway. These details, no doubt, are necessary to learn, but they are not the main point. More important is for the postulant to explore two questions: "Is this the way I want to love?" And, "Is this the way I want to make decisions?"

Another of my favorite analogies of incorporation into community is the method, as I have been told, by which a new queen bee is introduced into a hive. If she is simply placed in the hive, then the worker bees will kill her. Instead, a hole is made in the outer wall of the hive into which a lump of sugar is inserted. The worker bees will eat away the sugar from the inside of the hive, and the new queen, in her little box, will do the same from the outside. As the sugar lump becomes thinner and the two parties grow closer, they pick up each other's smell; by the time the sugar is fully eaten away, the queen and her subjects will accept one another. This analogy, like our own human courting process, illustrates how the new person and the community gradually come to know and accept one another. There is a subtle shift that signals the success of the incorporation process: at a certain point the postulant or novice begins to think and speak, not of "me and them," but of "us." At the same time, the community also begins to see him or her as "one of us."

Finally, it is painful but important to talk about what happens when, despite all hopes to the contrary, a mutual commitment can go sour. One of the most painful aspects of making a commitment to the shared life of a religious order, just as in making a commitment to marriage, is that vocations can end and relationships can die. This can happen after decades of marriage or after many years in the religious life. Like divorce, the breaking of a religious vow for life is tragic; nevertheless, it may sometimes be the most loving thing that can be done. If a relationship is dead, it is better to bury it.

It is vital that a community have a process for dispensation of the vow, whether it is one made annually or the vow made for life. Such a provision has not always been available in the past, and its lack has caused much psychological, financial, and social distress. Sometimes a temporary period of living outside a house of the order may precede a final separation, and may be helpful for both the individual and the community in making that decision. Such periods of partial separation should be constitutionally provided for; they have been designated extended service, leave of absence, suspension, detached service, monk not in residence, exclaustration, and a

number of other categories. Each has its own specifica-
tions. Some are initiated by the member, and some by
the community. Such separations may be temporary or
lifelong. All should have careful guidelines regarding
obligations both to the community and the member in
specifics such as duration, renewal, obedience, and
finance. Sometimes periods of separation lead to rein-
corporation, sometimes they are renewed at certain
intervals, and sometimes they lead to final dispensation
of the vow.

As in the case of divorce, the seriousness of severing
the vow made for life has led in the past, and in some
cases even now, to an unfortunate atmosphere of shame,
secrecy, and animosity. The dispensed member in that
scenario would lose contact with the community, never
"darkening its doors," and would not even be spoken of
again. A wonderful turning point in this deplorable situation happened when I was fairly new to the Order of
Saint Helena. A sister who had been in life vow for
many years and who had held positions of highest
authority chose to ask for dispensation of her vow and
leave community for a different way of life. The sister
had been deeply loved and respected, and consequently
her request was very traumatic for the community.
However, by grace the community responded with
compassion and courage. The sister was given support
and what practical help was available.

In addition, the community gathered at a Eucharistic
service which, while not a celebration of her separation,
was a liturgical recognition of the dispensation. At this
service, the departing sister returned the cross she had
received at life profession, and placed it on the altar. Her
Instrument of Profession, the paper she had signed when
she had made her life vow, was returned to her. At the

peace, she was told, "You are still our sister in Christ," and she was embraced by each member of the community. I believe everyone cried. I felt that those tears carried feelings of grief, disappointment, anger, compassion, joy for the new happiness to which she was entering, and (who knows?) perhaps even envy. At any rate, all feelings were able to be expressed and ritualized. This response of the community to her request for dispensation felt like coming out of the dark ages into the light. The liturgy signified not an approval of a promise broken, but a compassionate acceptance of reality.

+

CHAPTER THREE

Poverty, Chastity, and Obedience

When I first made my vow, it was understood quite differently than it is today. The change lies not so much in the theological meaning of the vow, but in the way it is lived out. When I entered religious life in "the old days," for example, our poverty was neither edifying nor especially spiritual—it was simply what we had always done even though the discipline no longer nourished us adequately. In some ways, our practices came close to being laughable. For instance, we never used the words "my" or "mine." I spoke of "our cell" even though that was the room in which only I slept; "our choir stall" even though I was the only one who sat in it; "our habit" though only I wore it. The ludicrousness of this practice surfaced one day when one of the sisters referred to "our dentures"! Poverty in those days meant that it was a great treat to walk down to the gate with another sister, or perhaps several times a year to have an ice cream cone.

Likewise, it was not so many decades ago when women and men religious were completely segregated in the name of chastity. When I first came to community, monks and nuns never ate together, and I was one of the first to experience the beginning of change in the early 1970s. Our sisters had been invited up to the Holy Cross monastery for the liturgy and meal of Maundy Thursday. We were warned that one of the older monks was particularly upset about women "infiltrating" the monks' refectory. As it happened, at that meal I was seated opposite this same venerable monk, and when the time came for conversation, lo and behold! he never stopped talking to me. He delighted in telling me a long story about how, when he was a novice, he raised goats on the lawn of the monastery!

The practice of obedience had similar contradictions in those days. Perhaps especially in the pre-Vatican II religious life, adult dependency and infantilism (and no doubt repressed rebellion) were not only tolerated but actually fostered. Mother and Father Superiors seemed to require a childish mode of obedience. There was a story about two sisters who had been to see a doctor (nuns always traveled in twos in those days) and were to be picked up by another sister at a certain time and place. The senior of the two nuns led them to the meeting place but the junior of the two offered tentatively that she thought it was meant to be on a corner two blocks away. The junior nun was right, but the senior insisted and they missed their ride, causing a good deal of trouble all around.

We have stories from the Middle Ages about novices who, in the name of obedience, were ordered to plant cabbages upside down, and to water dry sticks. Perhaps under the ridiculous aspect of these commands lay the same sort of logic that the Zen teachers exhibit in putting to their students koans such as "Think of the sound of one hand clapping": absurdity used as a way of freeing the mind from rigid adherence to being right for the sake of greater openness. In practice, however, I question just how freeing watering dry sticks actually was for many novices. This reminds me of my own first novitiate when I had an amusing experience with dry sticks. I was told to water some sweet pea seedlings that were trained around bamboo canes. It seemed to me a lost cause, but I didn't question and obeyed. Perhaps I overwatered them in my zeal for obedience; at any rate, as I knew they would, the sweet peas died. The dry bamboo sticks, however, like Aaron's rod, sprouted—an appropriate outcome for unthinking obedience!

Basic to any theory and practice of poverty, chastity, and obedience, ancient or modern, is the whole question of commitment—what, in fact does it mean to vow in the first place? The value of commitment seems to be especially open to question today. Why make any commitment? What is good about it? Once, when my nieces were teenagers, they asked me that question about their parents, who had been committed in a marriage vow for decades. When they asked their question we were at a family dinner, and I found myself looking at my wine glass. The analogy occurred to me that commitment is to love what the wine-making process is to grapes. In some ultimate sense wine is not *better* than grapes. But if you want good wine you need to take good grapes and trample them to mush and confine them together in a dark place for a long time, where they will go through all sorts of chemical changes and fermentation; then, if you are patient, you end up with a fine aged vintage. Without commitment to an exclusive love relationship, a person, so to speak, goes through life eating grapes, and never tasting the wine of a vintage love. There is a maturing that happens to love only when it is subjected to committed life together, in all its fermenting joys and sorrows, over a considerable period of time.

As in marriage, the monastic makes a public profession of commitment. In the case of the monastic, the vow is not made to another human being, or group of human beings, but to God. The vow is made to God in the context of the community and formularies of the religious order one is entering and not to specific members of that community. When I entered my present community at its largest convent, it was tempting to think that I would be committing myself to the particular sisters then resident there. However, five years later, when I made my life profession in that same convent's chapel, there was a different household; many of the original ones were stationed elsewhere, or had left the community, or in one case had died, and new ones had come. But even though there were different individual sisters in my household with whom to practice loving on a daily basis, the primary commitment to God and to the continuity of the order as a whole matured—fermented—as my vocation grew and deepened.

When I first made my vow, I confirmed what had been an inner choice with an outward profession. That profession has been a milestone for me on the continuing journey into the love of God. It identifies a significant choice of a particular value system, names and symbolizes it, and provides a means of remembering and living by it. I was given a great gift in the matter of choosing poverty, celibacy, and obedience. Before being professed in my present community I spent five years in an enclosed contemplative order. A few days before I was to enter, I was taken by a friend to hear Puccini's *La Bohéme* at the Metropolitan Opera. As the curtain rose on Act Three, and we heard the first notes of the overture, we saw a magnificent and quite realistic set of a snowfall at dawn, as a backdrop to the bohemian lovers' tragic lives. In that moment I was poignantly aware of my own years in Manhattan's West Village with my drama and writing friends, and was overwhelmed with nostalgia, both for the richness of that life I was leaving, and for the glory of this opera, the like of which I might never experience again. The blessing was that these beauties were not being wrested from me; I was giving them away of my own free will. I was able to delight in the past, present, and possible future good things of the life I had been living but at the same time choose to let them go for the sake of something I desired even more.

Making a commitment is a milestone on our journey, and is also the journey itself. In one sense the journey is chosen once and for all; in another sense it must be chosen continually. None of us finds it easy to live out our principles and moral values. There are two kinds of values—intrinsic and extrinsic—and when I was in college I became keenly aware of the difference. An extrinsic value for me was to get my degree and decent grades, which meant serious study; unfortunately at times a more attractive intrinsic value might take center stage, such as going out for pizza with friends or going to the movies. Another extrinsic value for me was mental alertness and safe driving, but often an intrinsic value was just one more drink. I found that if I decided *before* a party that I would have only two drinks, I might remember that decision when I had already had two drinks, and the third seemed harmless and inviting. In the same way, commitment is a choice made in full awareness that can help us delay gratification of an intrinsic desire for the purpose of serving an extrinsic good.

I have found that being faithful to the vow involves three essential things: first God's gift of grace, then self-discipline, and finally perseverance. This cooperation between God and a human being is analogous to the three aspects of artistic greatness. In art there needs first to be a God-given gift or talent; secondly, there needs to be the discipline of playing scales or exercise at the *barre* or painstaking life studies of the human body; and thirdly, there needs to be years of practice and of "finding one's own voice." Any two of these aspects without the third will result in a less-than-matured art. Without inborn talent there may be a great deal of production, but it will not be inspired; without discipline the work may be gifted, but not crafted into any major form; without perseverance the result may be "a flash in the pan." In the case of a religious vow lived to fulfillment, one must have the grace or vision of the call, the discipline of continually choosing what one perceives as the greater good, and the sheer perseverance of "hanging in there."

Often a vow is marked by a change of name. In the case of the marriage vow, it might be changing to or adding the name of the spouse, and in the religious vow it traditionally has been the adopting of the name of a saint or biblical character in exchange for or in addition to one's original or baptismal name. To some people this is a very welcome aspect of the call—it can signify a fresh start, a new chapter in their life. To others it seems abhorrent, almost as if their identity is being taken from them. Adding "Stephen" to my birth name, "Ellen," was a great gift and privilege for me as it was the name of the priest who baptized me and brought me to understand the Christian way of love. Adding "Stephen" did not in any way change my understanding of myself, but it gave me, so to speak, a banner to carry with me—a banner, as I read in the Song of Solomon, of love.

POVERTY

Poverty is to have no possessions of one's own, but to live in simplicity and thankfulness, holding all goods in common and being willing to share what we have.

Religious poverty used to mean having to ask permission for every tube of toothpaste, pair of socks, or watchband. Now, in many communities, sisters and brothers receive personal stipends—a modest monthly amount, usually under a hundred dollars, with which to buy personal items like shampoo and soap, haircuts and calendars, and all but major clothing (such as a new winter coat or shoes.) The modest amount is sufficient because we are given good used clothing by friends and associates, we have fine local thrift shops, and most of our needs are supplied by the community. Using what others no longer need seems like a kind of recycling, and recycling in all its forms is an important aspect of poverty today, as well as a witness against consumerism and waste. We have found new ways to live the vow of religious poverty. We do not have any property in our own name, but at the same time we are avoiding the unfortunate "Mother, may I?" climate so antipathetic to mature men and women in community.

Still, the culture shock of first encountering monastic poverty affects each newcomer to the religious life in a different way. Here's an example of one way it particularly affected me. When I first entered community life, the more or less generally accepted monastic décor could be described as straight-backed chairs, bare floors, and, except for the occasional holy picture, bare walls as well. One advantage of that style was that it created a kind of neutrality, so that sisters and guests could experience the convent or monastery as God's house, not rooms marked by the taste, much less the clutter, of any one particular personality. However, when our community thought about it in the early days of renewal, we realized that our common spaces could be neutral without being unattractive or uncomfortable. I remember the day when the superior of the men's Order of the Holy Cross, who was visiting in our reception room, said to us that upholstered chairs were just as holy as straight wooden ones! Believe it or not, at first that was something of a shock, but soon we changed to simple but more comfortable chairs.

With the positive aspects of that change came a challenge in regard to the ambience of our common areas. The convent and monastery are both home to those who live in them, and also a neutral welcoming space for visitors. Every person I know has very definite ideas about the décor they are comfortable with. "Homey" to one sister may mean frilly white curtains and flowered throw pillows. That doesn't signify home to me. Finding a common denominator for a dozen or so very diverse people and the guests to whom they offer hospitality can be a real challenge today. This may sound trivial, but one of the toughest parts of the initial experience of poverty for me was giving away my mother's Wedgwood black basalt demitasse cups and using mugs decorated with "cute" sayings or Christmas kitsch. I am sure it was good for my soul to realize what a culture snob I was, and to realize that a more profound poverty was not only giving away things I liked, but doing away with my critical attitude about what took their place.

Still, however, I struggle with the temptation to define myself by objects I use and prefer. In one sense my preferences and choices *are* part of who I am; they only become hindrances, and failures in holy poverty, when they lead me into being judgmental or rigid. The ultimate goal of spiritual poverty is freedom to be ourselves, without petty loves and hates, in whatever circumstances or environment we find ourselves. Saint Paul taught this: "I know what it is to have little, and I know what it is to have plenty. In any and all circumstances I have learned the secret of being well-fed and of going hungry, of having plenty and of being in need" (Philippians 4:12). Neurosis, which is opposed to the kind of holy freedom described by Saint Paul, has been called "wanting what you do not have, and hating what you've got."

It is not always easy to know what I really want—to identify my deepest desire, what is truly *worth*while. Our lives may be rich in the value that our culture places on commodities and services, but lacking in true worth. I had something of this feeling myself in the months before I identified my call to religious poverty. I felt surrounded by things of value—a fine education, a healthy body, enough money to live on, and my mother's Wedgwood demitasse cups! But where was my worth—the meaning to which I would commit myself? During that time I recalled the poignant story of King Midas. The legendary monarch was granted one day the wish that everything he touched would turn to gold. When evening came he discovered that his golden food was inedible, and that he would starve to death. He then begged the gods to withdraw his unwise request, and his plea was granted. Only then could he eat, or dare to touch the people he loved. Midas seems to have had to learn the hard way that the poor may lack valued commodities, but be rich in worth.

Poverty calls me to recognize the difference between true worth and culturally assigned value, and also the difference between acquiring a possession and receiving a gift. I am called to respect creation as gift because I am a creature fashioned in the image of a Creator who, in the deepest sense, respects the integrity of creation. Voluntary religious poverty imitates God's refusal to exploit or manipulate the natural world. It recognizes the beauty, the goodness, the sanctity of things. It does not reject or despise them; it receives them as the works and gift of God. In religious poverty I am called not to *possess* good things as if they were mine, nor to waste them, but to use them for God's glory. In recent years this respect for the sacredness of God's creation has joined forces with the new physics. John Polkinghorne, a quantum physicist who is also an Anglican priest, has offered us a splendid insight. He looks at reality through the eye of science and also though the eye of Christian faith. He claims that this "binocular vision" enables him to see much more profoundly than he could with either eye on its own. It is with this "binocular vision" of scientific and divine reality that we attempt to see the abundance of God's gifts to us in the natural world.

Our commitment to respect God's creation rather than possess or consume it has implications not only for the welfare of the natural world but also for that of our own souls. Evelyn Underhill wrote:

> We mostly spend [our] lives conjugating three
> verbs: to Want, to Have and to Do. Craving,
> clutching, and fussing, on the material, political,
> social, emotional, intellectual—even on the reli-
> gious—plane, we are kept in perpetual unrest: for-
> getting that none of these verbs have any ultimate
> significance, except so far as they are transcended
> by and included in, the fundamental verb, to Be:
> and that Being, not wanting, having and doing, is
> the essence of a spiritual life.[3]

It is all too easy, however, to identify myself by my possessions—even if technically I don't own them. We are
all prone to this. A former superior of our community
once made a visitation to one of the sisters who was
teaching and living at a school. This sister had the use of
a golf cart to get around the campus. On one occasion
the superior remarked to the sister that one of the tires
on her cart had gone flat, whereupon the latter became
very upset and took the remark as a personal criticism—
as if she did not know where her skin ended and the
cart began! I do understand that sister's feelings. Before
I entered my first religious community, I gave my
father's signet ring to my niece and I felt as if I might as
well have given away my little finger, as if I had given
away a part of myself.

It is important to remember that religious poverty is
not deprivation or indigence. The practices of *vowed*
poverty are designed to free us from exploitation of
earth's resources—and from the *affectation* of austerity as
well. In the enclosed community where I first lived, we
slept on mattresses of straw. The straw pallets had to be
renewed about once a year and were not even that
uncomfortable, if indeed that was part of the reason we

had them. I remember I once woke feeling something sharp, and in the morning found that a bit of wood with a nail in it had gotten mixed in among the straw, but otherwise the straw palettes were not much more than a nuisance and an anachronism. Buying new straw every year was even probably more expensive than buying a good mattress that would last a long time.

Today the way I practice holy poverty in the mattress department is very different and much more like the way any family living on a tight budget goes about it. A few years ago I noticed that the mattress I was sleeping on had given way along the sides and I was having to wake up often to turn back to the center. I felt as if I were in danger of rolling off the bed! I have a bad back and this nightly exercise, besides interrupting my sleep, became somewhat painful. So after finding that turning the mattress and trying an egg crate foam pad didn't help, I brought a request for a new mattress to our weekly house meeting. One sister suggested what kind of mattress she thought I needed, another how and where I might find it, and the sister who oversees our house budget checked that this was a possible time for the purchase. Discerning together about our individual and common needs, we try to practice a poverty that is neither indigence, nor indulgence; one that does not promote deprivation for deprivation's sake, but that, on the other hand, is also a witness against indiscriminate purchasing and luxury. The practice of poverty always needs to be reevaluated, taking into account the present time and culture. In a past age wooden bowls were used by the poor; now the equivalent items might be expensive affectations as well as potentially unsanitary.

We are called to serve the spirit of our vow, and the spirit leads us to ever new ways of practicing it. For example, there has been a recent trend of seeing a call to recycle as part of the good stewardship of the earth's natural resources, and to use products that will biodegrade effectively. In my community we buy products that have been made of recycled materials. We endeavor to serve food that is not as high on the food chain as might be usual for the culture around us, to be conscious of portion control and the creative use of leftovers, and to minimize the use of prepackaged foods. We are also creative in our recycling of the secular clothing we wear when we are not in our habits. People give us donations of clothes that have been worn, and those items the sisters cannot use we pass on to people who are indigent.

At this point you may be asking, "All very well, but in a *practical* way, how do you monastics support yourselves financially?" It is a good question, with a complex answer. Unlike many of the Roman Catholic religious communities, Anglican orders are not largely supported by diocesan funding. Some send out appeals, some have an endowment or a "quasi-endowment," many have a profitable guest ministry; most employ a mixture of these means, along with other innovative measures. One community houses a cell-phone tower on their property, the income from which pays their operating expenses. My own community depends mainly on the gifts of friends and associates. The gifts range from quite small to quite large, and the large gifts and bequests are invested with a care for good stewardship, and attention to social concerns; for instance, we do not invest in military interests or tobacco products. We cannot, however, live solely on the income from these invested gifts, and we depend on various other sources. Besides gifts and donations that we continue to receive, we derive considerable income from ministries of hospitality in two of our houses. Also, sisters receive honoraria in exchange for their individual ministries. Our ministries are varied; they include a variety of parish work by both our ordained and lay sisters, and clergy supply; teaching, preaching, and leading retreats, quiet days, and conferences; psychotherapy and spiritual direction; hospital chaplaincy; work with the urban poor and homeless; the writing of books and icons; and the creation of a great variety of crafts that we offer for suggested donations in our houses. We also receive income from planned giving, from response to appeals, and from occasional parish-designated funding. A few sisters have part-time salaried jobs that are paid into the order's funds.

And because we believe that our vow must be truly chosen, each sister chooses to add her own individual practice of poverty. One sister, for example, washes and irons her handkerchiefs rather than use the tissues that would cost the community money and the earth its trees. Others produce original cards for special celebrations rather than buying them. Some sisters choose to walk short distances rather than drive for reasons of frugality, as well as for health. One of my small contributions is turning lights and dripping faucets off—and trying my best not to give in to the temptation of assuming that I'm the only one who does!

Spiritual poverty may be seen as freedom to have or not to have. Even beyond Saint Paul's stripping down for his ministry is his life as total gift. He is not only the Olympic runner but also the libation to the gods—to God. "As for me, I am already being poured out as a libation, and the time of my departure has come. I have fought the good fight, I have finished the race, I have kept the faith" (2 Timothy 4:6–7). Following Jesus and

Paul, other saints, notably Francis of Assisi, have lived and taught that the joy involved in spiritual poverty is a mutual love gift between God and the human soul. Once again we remember the caveat: if we do not have a strong sense of self, we cannot "deny" ourselves or spend ourselves in the service of a greater cause. First the sense of self must be nurtured and strengthened; *then* it may be given or given up for the greater goods of spiritual freedom and bringing in the reign of God.

CHASTITY

Chastity means to root in God our power to love, and to live in the single celibate state to express that love in divine worship and in service to others.

Why would anyone choose to be celibate? Wouldn't it be much better to have a loving partner? Isn't the only good reason for a person to be celibate that she or he just can't find a partner? Isn't celibate chastity against healthy human nature? These are questions I have heard since the idea of living as a celibate person first entered my head. In response, I, and many other people I know, have found that celibacy is a fulfilling and complementary choice to sexual partnership. But, just as in choosing a human partner, there are as many reasons and motives for choosing celibate chastity as there are persons who do so. Every nun or monk who chooses to live in celibate chastity has not only a unique call to this way of expressing love, but different motives for the choice. Every one of us has a unique psycho-sexual history. This personal history is carried with us into the way we come to choose and live this aspect of the threefold vow.

I know of one monk, for instance, who had had a very troubled and lonesome childhood, and who came to the monastery seeking a loving and accepting community. I know of a sister who survived an abusive marriage and came seeking community as a safe context for love and service. I know of a friar whose youth was spent in a particularly repressive time and place and whose attraction to other men prevented him from having an open, committed partnership; fleeing contempt and condemnation, he came looking for an accepting community. I know of a nun who as a teenager had had a vision of Christ calling her to be his own beloved. I know of others coming to community on the rebound from failed affairs, or simply to get away from home. Reasons for choosing celibate community are diverse and complex. Some of these motives might be called "noble," such as the desire to love God and serve God's people; some, like those just cited, are perhaps less noble but completely human and understandable. The marvelous thing is that God's grace can take any and all motives, and, with human cooperation, craft good vocations out of them.

The only example of the call to celibacy from a unique psycho-sexual history of which I am aware in any depth is, of course, my own. To sketch in the bare skeleton of it here may serve in some small measure to show how the call may be heard and explored amid the noise of the prevailing culture and the convolutions of the human heart.

My father, to whom I was close, died when I was thirteen and I resented and feared my mother's new unilateral power. My mother did not have a vocation to motherhood; near the end of her life she told me that what she had really wanted to do with her life was to be editor of *The New York Times*! From very early years I had the feeling that my mother's values—of a successful marriage, social status, beauty, wealth, sophistication, and mental brilliance (she was *Phi Beta Kappa* in college, and received an MA in philosophy at Columbia)—were ones that I probably could not, and certainly did not want to emulate. On the contrary, I rebelled against those values. I had been a very anxious child; if my mother's values were sane, then I was either a failure or crazy—or both. I was not only anxious, I was starved for affection and affirmation. From the time my father died, I started unconsciously looking for a replacement who would sweep me up in his big strong arms and tell me I was special. Needless to say, no male high school or college student could fulfill or cope with these unspoken but compelling demands. One by one they withdrew, while women friends as well were often put off by my intensity.

Accordingly, I developed two perceptions of myself with which I lived long before they became conscious enough to be named. They were the "Little Orphan Waif," who desperately needed the affirming and affectionate parent figure, and the "Queen of Sheba," who didn't need anybody, thank you very much. I spent the decades of my youth flipping back and forth between these perceptions of myself and acting out of them. I was by turns frantically trying to find the man who would make me feel safe and okay, and then, when I felt myself losing any self-esteem I had, by withdrawing and feeling, "I don't need them—they wouldn't understand anyway." The sexual component of my being was correspondingly passionate or frigid.

Then, in college, through a series of courses in religion, I met Jesus. I was an English major and I remember thinking, "If this character Jesus is not who the scripture says he is—if he is a literary creation—who wrote him? He is certainly a greater character than Hamlet, and which of those fishermen or tax collectors who recorded his words and actions was greater than Shakespeare?" Eventually I became intellectually converted, but I knew somehow that full conversion would mean surrender—would mean no longer being "the master of my fate" and "the captain of my soul," as I somewhat dramatically thought of it. Eight years after I was intellectually converted, I did surrender. Baptism changed me in every dimension of my being, including my sexuality. I no longer felt driven—in a sense, I had found "Daddy." God was the one who would sweep me up in the everlasting arms and tell me how special and lovable I was. Jesus was both strong enough to make me feel affirmed and secure, and also, as I have said, was "the truth."

Shortly after I was baptized, in my late twenties, I met a man a few years younger than I who was very physically attractive and mentally my peer. We could and did talk about everything. We fell in love. In my new sense of myself as a Christian I resisted sexual intercourse, and he gladly respected this. After a year's engagement we were married in the Episcopal Church, but for reasons concerning my husband's sexuality, of which he had not been fully conscious when we were engaged, the marriage was never consummated. We still loved one another—and stayed together for three years. Those years were extremely painful for us both, and at the end of them his guilt and frustration began to manifest itself in acts of physical violence toward me. With wise counsel, and by mutual consent, we parted. I obtained a civil divorce, and subsequently an ecclesiastical annulment. I did not care to marry anyone else, and I no longer cared to date casually. Not long after we parted, I heard and finally responded to the call to try my vocation in religious life.

After the marriage ended and before I entered community, I had been living as a single woman; I had no "significant other." As a novice, I gradually became aware of the difference between singleness and celibacy; there was a real sense in which God became my significant other. In another sense, community was my significant other as well—moving through the stages of postulancy, novitiate, and then profession is a process of deepening commitment. As two lovers gradually deepen their commitment to one another, so do men and women who are coming into community. This deepening relationship to God in prayer, and to the members of my community in relationship, can be called the *vertical* and the *horizontal* aspects of commitment—the love of God and the love of neighbor. At some times monastics experience the intensity of this daily growth in love with their significant others as joy and at other times as painful challenge, but always as a cross where the vertical and horizontal loves intersect.

When I feel a sense of ordinary human loneliness in community, it is often because I did not pick these women I live with. We are not one another's "type" and do not have the same way of looking at life; we do not have that much in common to talk about, and they would not be the friends I would choose living on my own. For this reason I turn to God, who has indeed picked them for me! On the other hand, when my prayer is "dry" and I don't sense God's presence, my sisters are there for me. Even if we don't share many of each others' particular interests such as math puzzles or bird watching or poetry, murder mysteries or grandchildren, we are committed to support one another.

The celibate life depends on both the "vertical" dimension of prayer and on the "horizontal" intercourse of community.

However, to many people celibacy does seem merely to be part of the "package" of religious life, and an odd, if not bizarre part at that. A number of people have asked me, "If Anglican priests can marry, can't you sisters marry?" This seems at first to be a reasonable question. But the answer is, of course, "no." In the past priests were designated either "regular"—those who lived under monastic rule (Latin, *regula*)—or "secular"—those whose obedience was within the diocesan structure. The monastic, whether male or female, Catholic or Protestant, ordained or not, has always been and still is celibate. It is not a question of whether a monk or nun can marry; rather the choice not to marry is fundamental to the monastic call. A traditional religious community is a context that gives relational and social context to a call to celibacy. That, of course, is not its only reason for being, but it is an important one.

It seems a good deal easier now to discuss human sexuality in a monastic context than when I entered forty years ago. Then, I received a vague impression that nuns didn't have sexuality or bodies—almost that they didn't have legs or hair, or if they did, such things were not to be discussed, much less seen! Even now, monastic sexuality—and monastics, like all humankind, *are* sexual beings—is perhaps still the most difficult aspect of the vow to talk about in depth and in particulars. But it needs to be spoken of because our human sexuality is a profound part of our human being and closely connected to our spirituality; both sexuality and spirituality are rooted in the way in which we love.

Bonnell Spencer of the Order of the Holy Cross, a monastic pioneer in researching celibate chastity, has described it as reverence for the integrity of other people. Chastity refrains from exploiting or using persons as objects, and it respects to the full the individuality of the other. Celibate chastity in no way involves a fear, repudiation, or repression of sex. Celibate persons try to remember that they are called to a love relationship with as many persons as possible, not just with those for whom they feel a physical, emotional, intellectual, or spiritual attraction. Perhaps the basic sin against chastity is the exploitation of others, though overt sexual abuse is only one form of such exploitation; we can also exploit others in our relationships with them through possessiveness and desire to dominate without ever touching them.

Before a celibate person reaches the admirable state of bringing compassionate love to every human encounter, he or she often experiences an exclusive one-to-one sexual attraction. If such a relationship has not involved exploitation of one of the parties, or a decision for genital consummation, it may well be a helpful stage in the growth toward celibate maturity. If we have not learned how to love one person in particular, it will be difficult to love many people "in general." When I first came to community, the thought of loving all these senior sisters was daunting. Some of them seemed forbidding, others too busy to be available, and others, frankly, seemed unlovable. Not long after I was a novice, I was sent on a teaching mission with a novice brother of a men's community. What I experienced in our getting to know one another was not what I had known before as "love" in a romantic sense, but instead I had found a "buddy," a friend on the journey. Somehow that special monastic friendship helped me begin to love my sisters a little better.

Sometimes it is hard to discern the exact line between romantic and sisterly or brotherly love. When does an affectionate handclasp move into an erotic invitation? Statistics on the matter of sexual activity of any kind in celibate communities are hard to come by and not very specific. Somewhere at a conference years ago I took notes on what was termed "The Touch Scale." It has been clarifying and useful to me. My own modification of the Touch Scale runs as follows:

1. The touch of affection—which might be bestowed on a puppy dog as well as a human being;

2. The touch of caring—which one might offer to a patient in the hospital, or as healing touch;

3. The ritual touch—as at the exchange of the peace at the Eucharist or at anointing;

4. The touch of trust—supporting another's weakness, or a medical practitioner's examination;

5. The touch of attraction, physical or spiritual—holding hands, a light kiss, a brief hug;

6. The erotic touch—that which carries physical desire; and

7. The genital touch—that which initiates genital activity.

I would venture that a violation of chastity might fall somewhere between erotic and genital contact. Of course, a touch may be offered to the other in the spirit and with the intent of affection or trust, and unpredictably arouse an erotic response. One can only be careful of one's intentions.

The erotic touching of oneself, or masturbation, has its own scale. I have come across statements from people of some authority that define masturbation on a spectrum that ranges from a lesser sin to being no different than scratching one's ear; or from a neurotic addiction to an occasional gift of pleasure to oneself. The question of whether or to what extent the act violates celibate chastity perhaps is best left to the individual soul and God.

The celibate state has always been seen from two major perspectives: the practical and the spiritual. First, we have Saint Paul's metaphor of the Olympic runner—the "stripping down" appropriate to discipleship and ministry. Many people see the prime value of celibacy as lying in the freedom to go where one is called. This view has validity; in a sense celibacy is an emotional and practical stripping down and "traveling light" for the sake of the gospel. A person free of primary attachment to a partner, spouse, aged parent, or child is more emotionally and ethically free to respond wherever and whenever the call to ministry comes: "Here I am, send me."

Being thus unencumbered applies both to the freedom to go and to be available when others come. When I am listening to or speaking with others, either away or at home, in that moment *they* become my "significant other." There is no other human being to whom I will return at the end of the day, to whom I owe my primary human allegiance. This life condition has been very helpful and freeing to me in establishing trust and confidentiality with those who come to speak to me, and to those to whom I go on mission. It is as if Jesus had said to me: "No bag for your journey, or two tunics, or sandals, or a staff," and then added, "or a cell phone to call home on!" (To be honest, some of our sisters do carry cell phones, and carry bags on mission, and, I, alas, have accumulated many more "tunics and sandals" than I need!) We strive, however, each as we are able, to live into the stripped down "freedom of the glory of the children of God."

Besides the practical consideration of freeing us for personal encounter and ministry, celibacy is, in the second place, a way to love—a different outlet for our sexual and spiritual energies. As in any way of loving, celibacy is about becoming, as Saint Irenaeus wrote, "a human being fully alive." To the extent that we know and love ourselves as human beings fully alive, can we give ourselves in love to others.

It is perhaps inevitable that the followers of Christ have traditionally attached the nuptial metaphor to the celibate lifestyle. Scripturally the church is the "Bride of Christ," and the term has been interpreted to refer to the mystical union of Christ and the individual human soul by such saints as Teresa of Avila, Catherine of Siena, and John of the Cross. However, because the bridal image has in recent centuries been badly sentimentalized and trivialized, especially in regard to nuns, it is distasteful today—novices no longer wear frilly white wedding dresses at their "clothing" ceremonies!

In these times it is probably useful to avoid using the terms "nuptial," "marriage," and "bride" in referring to monastic chastity. However, I have heard a great number of people describing how they began to think about becoming a monastic, and the metaphor of an intimate and in a sense exclusive love relationship to God figured in most cases. In any significant love relationship the particulars of the relational history of both parties, the initial attraction, and the milestones of intimacy are unique. The specific ways that one can awaken to a committed relationship of love with God are at least as particular as in any human-to-human love relationship. Here, again, is an illustration from my own life story, a milestone on my journey with God.

Once, when I was at my lowest spiritual ebb—the very worst time of confusion and pain in my loving but unconsummated marriage—God came to me in that depth. My husband and I were staying in a little rented apartment on the edge of a city, on one of those desolate streets lined with used car lots and storehouses. It was October, and the pavement was spattered with damp rusty brown leaves. Incongruously, there was a small church there, once white but now smudged with the exhaust fumes of the neighborhood and blown leaves. One Sunday morning when my husband was working, I walked to the little church and went in. I thought I was just in time for the service, but the church was empty. I waited. No one came. After I had silently cried out all the prayers I knew how to say, I just knelt there, my soul in pain and my mind a blank. Then, suddenly, before me was light, and in the light, or of it, was a face smiling with infinite compassion, and the smile seemed to say, "I know." Then I was alone again and I realized that it had been the face of Jesus. I don't know how long I stayed there, but then people started coming into the church and soon the service began. Somewhere in the middle of the service I realized that in my distress I had not registered that this was the morning that daylight savings time ended, and I hadn't changed my watch! I had come an hour too early by earth time, *chronos*, but just right for *kairos*, God's cosmic time. I have never minded that no consolation quite like that ever happened to me again; I never again needed it as I had that day.

In my experience God is very economic. As I have been called to more and more mature loving, I have been given what I have needed, but just that. I have had to realize in my own body, mind, and spirit that the gate is narrow and the road is hard that leads to life. The road less traveled is full of ruts and potholes. I have been asked, "What if a vowed monastic stumbles? What if the promise of chastity is broken?" There is a saying in the lore: "Saints are not people who never fall, they are people who pick themselves up and carry on." When temptation appears, there is always a new choice to be made for one's vowed life.

A sister once told me a story about a sexual temptation that had the outcome of strengthening her vow. She was stationed in a small convent—"a branch house"— where several local priests came on various days of the week to celebrate the Eucharist for them. One of these priests was an attractive married man who made a practice of talking at the breakfast table after mass about the readings for the next Sunday, gathering ideas for his coming sermon. The sister who told the story found herself on the same wavelength as this priest both theologically and spiritually, and their breakfast interchanges became quite illuminating. Eventually the sister and the priest, being self-aware people, acknowledged that an erotic dimension had come into their relationship. One day, in a private conference, they found themselves embracing. The sister reported that she had said in a half-jesting way something like: "If only we could consummate this love just once, and then continue to be true to our other vows!" But the priest replied that for his part once would not be acceptable—he wanted a love affair. At that point the sister visualized all the lies and pain and confusion and harm to others that would attend such a self-pleasing act, even if only committed once, and she chose to say "no."

There is a story about Saint Francis (possibly apocryphal) that has been comforting and supportive to me in using reason against strong temptation. Once Francis was undergoing a severe temptation to break his vow of chastity. He tried fasting and discipline but the temptation did not go away. He refrained from beating himself with a whip because he did not want to damage his habit. It was very cold and there was snow up in the Italian mountains where they were making a retreat. Francis went outside and built himself a snowman. Then next to it he built a snow-woman, and said: "There you are, Francis, and there is your lovely wife." Then he built two snow-children: "There are your dear children!" And then, to serve his growing family, he built two snowmen for servants. Then he said: "There is your family, Francis. Is that really your vocation?" And he made the choice once again for celibacy. And do you know what? By that time the temptation had gone!

The vow may be said to act as an anchor to hold against the storms of temptation, but it is a mistake to believe that professing a vow that includes celibate chastity is an infallible protection against human sexual desires and temptations. The habit of a monastic is not necessarily a deterrent to eroticism, and in fact may make the monastic especially attractive to certain people. In my own years of living under the vow, four priests, at different times and places, have made serious sexual advances to me, most often in the sacristy before or after the Eucharist. Perhaps erroneously, I felt that I could not say anything about these incidents, and they were disturbing. In one of the cases the attraction became mutual, not unlike the story of the sister and the priest above, and that was very disturbing indeed. I was in my fifties and had felt safely beyond any emotional tempests, but the storm arose, and the anchor was not holding. By God's grace and my own cooperation I, too, did not consent to the consummation of this attraction, but I learned a hard lesson: even after decades of profession I could not *use* my vow for protection, I had once again to *choose* my vow. This hard continuing need to choose to live one's vow requires attention and prayer.

Our sexuality, even if it is not active, as in the case of a monastic, must mature with the rest of the whole human being and become integrated in order for the whole person to move through the constriction of the narrow gate into the liberty of "a human being fully alive." A person's image of herself or himself as a sexual being is perhaps one of the most basic and most persistent of images, but it is usually one of many. All of the images we have of ourselves may be recognized and then put in their places as not *in themselves* defining us. A sense of humor is helpful. One Christmas, in gratitude for the healing and integration I was experiencing through God's grace and the psychotherapy with which my community's encouragement (and insurance) had gifted me, I made my therapist a Christmas card. Around a decorated tree I painted all the images of myself that we had uncovered together. Besides the Needy Orphan Waif, and the Queen of Sheba, I painted the hideous little murderer whom I had met in a dream, the seductive sex object, the holy nun, the famous dramatist, the playful dolphin, the ravening wolf, and the wise old crone.

Then I painted a holly-festooned banner above the tree with the caption, "Merry Christmas from all of us!"

OBEDIENCE

Obedience is to be open to the will of God as it is heard not only in one's prayer, but also in the insights of others and in the common mind of the community.

Once, when I was about to leave London and return to the United States, I asked my mentor and priest a question: "If someday in the future I am in a terrible spot, and you are not around, can you give me something—a word—to remember and turn to?" Without any hesitation he said: "Obedience." Well, for years I thought he meant something like, "Look around for someone else to be obedient to." More recently, however, I have felt fairly sure that that is not what he meant at all. It was more like, "Get focused, open yourself to God, and *listen.*"

Obedience is a call to listen, and to respond in love. It comes from two Latin roots: *ob* + *audire,* meaning "to hear." (From *audire* we derive such words as "auditory" and "auditorium.") It is further interesting to note that the Greek word meaning "to hear" is also associated with obedience; from the Greek root ακουω, to hear, we derive "acoustics." In his letter to the church in Philippi, Saint Paul uses ακουω to mean obedience: Jesus "humbled himself and became *obedient* (ὑπήκοοσ) to the point of death—even death on a cross" (Philippians 2:8). And in Hebrew there is the word *shema,* as in "Hear, O Israel." To hear with our inner as well as our outer ears means to be open to obey. We can therefore see this third aspect of the vow as a commitment to listen, to trust, to surrender what is fearful and controlling in ourselves, and to listen to the deepest desires of our own hearts.

Even though renewal and liberation have changed how we live the vow today, to make a commitment to obedience is one of life's bigger and riskier steps. Any surrender of one's own way and will is good news *only* when it is done for the sake of greater life, freedom, and joy. A friend of mine once pointed out in his sermon at a sister's life profession that when a woman marries John, she gives up all potential intimacy with, for instance, Stephen and Bill—not for the sake of renouncing Stephen and Bill, but for the joy of making a primary commitment to John. As we commit ourselves to God as our primary "significant other," we hear our particular call, and choose to make a commitment to holy obedience.

However, obedience is still difficult to understand, and many of us are not skilled in listening to one another. There is good reason to be wary of vowing obedience to any community or group. In "the bad old days" of religious life, even as recently as my own first years under vow, fear was built into obedience. It involved asking permission for almost everything. I remember being at a gathering of religious back then when one sister hurried across a wide lawn to ask the superior if she could wheel an infirm sister into the dining area! The prevailing fear was that you would ask something and be told "no" and that would be not only disappointing but humiliating. For many it would reawaken painful experiences in childhood when desires were refused or trivialized.

In my own community we have worked hard at freeing ourselves from the "Mother, may I?" syndrome, but at times I too have had to reach beyond my own wishes in order to obey. When in the 1980s Saint Helena had four convents, the superior asked each of us to list in order of preference where we would wish to be stationed. On my list the convent in Seattle, Washington, came in last; I very much wanted to stay in the East where I was born and grew up. I felt a twinge of fear that having asked, I might not get what I wanted, and as it turned out I *was* asked to go to Seattle, and in fact spent ten years there. I never came to feel completely acclimated, but those ten years turned out to be perhaps the most formative decade of my life.

I don't remember asking for anything else that was denied me, but I do remember being sometimes afraid to ask. When my mentor, Father Langton, was in his last illness, it seemed risky to ask if I might travel to England to see him one more time, but I did. To my amazement and delight, my community supported my going, and the superior even resurrected one of her own "travel habits," which were black rather than our usual white, in case I didn't have ready access to a washing machine! My gratitude for that experience helped me encourage others to ask in turn. I remember a younger sister who wanted to take a course in spiritual direction that would involve the cost of tuition and travel as well as time away from her responsibilities at home. This was not a usual request in those days. She confided to me something like, "the Advisory Council will never agree for that." I replied: "*Your* job is to discern whether this is something you *really* feel called to, and then ask; *Council's* job is to discern whether the community can afford the cost and your time away." In the end, the answer was once again "yes."

I had to attain a certain level of maturity before I could be obedient in a healthy way. I needed to have enough easiness in myself that I could be open to another person's or the community's sense of what was right. I know some religious who have had an even harder time with healthy obedience than I did. Some have been harshly denied what they desired, even what they needed; others have grown up under a system of inconsistent reward and punishment, or have experienced traumatizing physical or emotional abuse. People with these histories can have a long road of healing to travel before they can come to a sense that holy obedience is good news. If you have been a victim, or treated like an object or a slave, obedience can feel *un*holy. Resistance and *dis*obedience may be a step forward for many such oppressed persons. The formula of human development from dependence through counterdependence to interdependence sounds rather simplistic, yet it describes a human reality. The infant, who is properly dependent, becomes the teenager whose journey to independence often looks like rebellion, but who may grow into the interdependence of psycho-spiritual maturity in due time. Unfortunately this process does not always follow the appropriate chronology; if development is blocked by early trauma, some dependency and/or resistance may be manifest in persons chronologically adult. In fact most of us tend, unlike Saint Paul, not to have put away all our childish things.

It is small wonder that when inappropriate dependence is removed in a community's practice, independence hastens to fill the void. The rebel cry of independence is: "Nobody is going to tell me what to do ever again!" We need to experience power before we can choose to surrender it. A number of women have said to me that they cannot cope with the Christian theology of surrender—as, for example, "Deny yourself." They have been denied too long, and now they want a theology that allows them to fulfill themselves. The interesting thing is that men also have told me that they do not know how to cope with a theology of surrender; all their upbringing was to win and achieve and succeed. Perhaps it comes round once more to our theme song: a vessel must be filled before it can be poured from; a self must be esteemed—fulfilled—before it can rightly be surrendered or denied.

Many of the horror stories of inappropriate religious obedience arose out of an ideal of radical self-giving to which only a few may be called, but which was held up as a norm for all. Holding up an ideal is one thing; imposing it as a rule is another. In the spiritual life one size never fits all. No doubt there are souls so filled to overflowing with God's grace (along with a realistic concept of self) that they never lose their serenity no matter what they are asked to do or where they find themselves. All very well for those who can practice such free willingness without doing violence to their psychic health. However, in any case, it is most important to protect conscience and justice. In his Rule for his brethren Saint Francis writes: "But should any of the ministers command any of the brothers to do something contrary to our life or against his conscience, he is not bound to obey him, since that is not obedience in which a fault or sin is committed."[4] No obedience that is holy is "blind obedience." We are always called to awareness, to conscience, and to choice.

What about conscience? What is it? I sometimes think of conscience as a *kibitzer* in a poker game. Say I am holding a three, four, six, and seven, and am tempted to draw one card to fill my inside straight. The *kibitzer* looking over my shoulder says that to draw to an inside straight is insane—the odds are astronomical against my drawing the right card. But my *will* is the function that makes the decision—either to obey the *kibitzer's* advice and fold my hand, or to go ahead and draw to the inside straight anyway. Informing my conscience might mean reading a book giving the exact odds in poker, or it might mean listening to the advice of my brother, who is a good poker player.

Obedience may often be misunderstood, distorted, or trivialized, but it has a very profound place in the religious life, and indeed in the human condition. It may well be the hardest work of the human spirit. To be mature and free we must obey—God, our own conscience, and those with rightful responsibility and authority. Our obedience, to be holy, must come from love and choice and not out of ignorance or fear.

About twenty years ago I learned a basic lesson in spiritual maturity through a crisis of obedience. When I was asked to go to Seattle to be in charge of our convent there, it coincided with a loss—I was not elected to a position I felt I was called to. This felt like a severe rejection that brought back the rejections of my childhood. A sabbatical time for which I had planned became a month's silent retreat. I took with me W. H. Longridge's classic Anglican interpretation of Saint Ignatius's *Spiritual Exercises.* Foolishly I had not asked for a spiritual director on the retreat, so I had no director except the Holy Spirit. When I came to the second week of the *Exercises,* called "the election," my spirit came to a screeching halt. There it was, in black and white: "I desire and choose poverty with Christ poor rather than riches; reproaches with Christ laden therewith, rather than honour; and I desire to be counted as worthless and a fool for Christ... rather than wise and prudent."[5] Whoa! *Choose* reproaches and human disregard? Impossible! What was good news about that? I read the passage over and over for a number of days, and cried. Why would I choose humiliation and rejection? I tried first to convince myself that the reason to accept rejection was that it was reality—I really was rejectable. Always had been.

Then the Holy Spirit (or my own right reason) whispered to me that was *not* a good reason! I prayed and cried some more and came up with another reason to accept reproach and rejection: if I accepted them first, then "they" couldn't hurt me with their rejection of me. The Holy Spirit whispered to me that this was an even worse reason. After I had prayed and despaired some more, I remembered a passage from Saint Paul, "I know what it is to have little, and I know what it is to have plenty. In any and all circumstances I have learned the secret of being well-fed and of going hungry, of having plenty and of being in need" (Philippians 4:12). Now *that* sounded like the kind of freedom I longed for. I knew that I thrived on praise, affirmation, and acceptance. Maybe to balance the scales I should choose to learn how to cope with reproach, humiliation, and rejection, so that "in any and all circumstances" I could live freely in the moment. I could practice the hard things in order to build up my spiritual muscles so that *however* others saw me I would not lose my own sense of who I am. Whatever the fallacy of that logic might be, it enabled me to *choose* to be obedient in that situation, and not take on the role of a victim.

When I first took the monastic vow for life I understood it as a binding commitment to God in the context of the Order of Saint Helena. Over the decades of living the vow I know that still to be true, but far more profoundly I have come to treasure my vowed life as the means to personal maturity, integration, and spiritual freedom.

CHAPTER FOUR

Life Together

My first community was headed by a superior whose wish, and sometimes whose whim, was my command. For example, when I was clothed in that community I did not have a choice as to my new name but was simply told that I would be called "Sister Mary Ancilla Domini," or "handmaid of the Lord." (It happened that the Roman Catholic Poor Clares in another city had a sister with that name, and our superior wanted one in hers.) I didn't like my new name. For one thing, I didn't see myself as a *maid,* and for another it seemed a bit heavy to bear the same name as Mary the mother of God. The name, though it had its origins in Mary's great song of praise, the *Magnificat,* also had its ridiculous aspect: people on the telephone and in doctor's offices invariably asked, "Sister Mary Ann *who?*" or called me "Sister Dominic," to say nothing of the fact that the initials spelled "MAD," which I may well have been at the time. But my understanding of obedience then was more than a bit skewed, so I didn't voice my discontent, and submitted to bearing that name for five years.

That community was an enclosed contemplative order, and in my time there it never exceeded six or seven members. We ate together, but in silence; we prayed, either alone or in choir, with our eyes on our breviaries; we lived together without speaking much to one another and, as much as possible, without making eye contact (an old custom called "custody of the eyes"). There was a brief time of recreation once a week that consisted of taking our supper on a tray to the room where the television was (it was the only time we watched it) and eating the meal during that week's episode of "Lassie." In other words, we had no chance at recreation to chat or to talk to one another about how the week had gone for us.

To be fair, I do remember a few instances of relationship that approached affection in that community. Occasionally the superior asked me to cut her hair in the evening. Without her veil and wimple she seemed to become human and vulnerable, and at those times we often exchanged a few sentences as women rather than as superior and novice or junior. Also, I had friendly moments, constricted though they were, with the only other young woman in the community. Sometimes we would snatch a few minutes from our prayers and chores to sit on the old wooden steps leading out to a back courtyard, where she introduced me to her favorite hymns in the 1940 Hymnal and I introduced her to the novels of Charles Dickens. But such moments were rare. From stories I have heard, the same sort of emotional distance was true in many other communities.

This practice of monastic reserve is a far cry from the view of relationships put forward in Aelred of Rievaulx's famous twelfth-century treatise on "spiritual friendship." As novice master and then abbot of a house of the austere Cistercian order, Aelred was long remembered for his extraordinary patience and tenderness with the brothers under his care. Aelred encouraged his monks to feel affection for one another. He wrote:

> But what happiness, what security, what joy to have someone to whom you dare to speak on terms of equality as to another self; one to whom you need have no fear to confess your failings; one to whom you can unblushingly make known what progress you have made in the spiritual life; one to whom you can entrust all the secrets of your heart.[6]

Moreover, Walter Daniel, Aelred's contemporary biographer, wrote of him that unlike some other abbots, Aelred was not scandalized by demonstrations of affection, such as holding hands, by his monks.[7] Yet in this respect his community was an appealing exception, and it took centuries for most men and women religious again to express happiness and affection in personal relationship by holding hands or hugging one another as an accepted form of greeting.

From the time of Pachomius's protocommunity in the third century right down to many contemporary orders, religious life has been structured so that each member's relationship to the others involved a primary relationship to a hierarchical superior—abbot, abbess, prior, guardian, mother or father superior. Perhaps some interaction or "bonding" happened among a group of novices, but it was limited and circumscribed; rarely could it be called friendship or emotional support. Too often there existed a kind of subtle competition that might be likened to sibling rivalry: which novices were most favored by the superior and life professed brothers or sisters?

When I entered the Order of Saint Helena, we novices were assigned our own common room in the basement and told we might decorate it. As this was in the early 1970s, there appeared on the walls a great many rainbows, doves, hearts and "alleluias." In a fit of rebellion, I took over a corner of the room and put up a large cross and a small figure kneeling beneath it with the caption, "There is always room at the bottom." Over the cross I posted a banner that read, "Deny yourself, it's later than you think!" This defiant attempt at humor was not well received, particularly by the most senior novice, who was very bright and a rather intimidating individual, to me. One day I was sewing a banner with a brown corduroy cross on a background of black cloak material. The lettering was a phrase from our old Rule: "No Tabor Without Calvary." Tabor was the mountain of the transfiguration of Christ, and Calvary that of the crucifixion, so that the meaning was, I suppose, something like, "If you can't bear the cross, you can't wear the crown." The senior novice, passing by, murmured sarcastically, "Cheerful banner you've got there!" I replied, "Yes, it expresses my personality." She scoffed, "I know—light black on dark black with purple fringe!" Though this could not be called a friendly exchange, it was, in fact, more of a lively personal interaction between sisters than was usual at that time. Decades later, our lives had taken different paths but the relationship had survived and become friendly. She sent me a postcard from the Holy Land with a photograph of Mount Tabor. On the back she had written, "I want you to know I visited Calvary first!" That was the kind of loving and easy bantering I missed those first years of my life in community. Back then the other sisters not only seemed distant, they seemed to me, most of the time, very serious.

The top-down hierarchical structure and potential for rivalry too often could infantilize newer sisters. For example, as a novice under this old regime I developed a severe pain in my neck—perhaps the novitiate experience *was* "a pain in the neck"! Following the rules, I took the problem to the novitiate director, who referred me to the infirmarian (the sister in charge of medical needs) and she in her turn helped me make an appointment with an orthopedist. No doubt the novitiate director also reported to the superior about my condition! Now we all find our own doctors and make our own appointments.

When young men and women entered religious establishments a century ago, many were teenagers with practically no life experience, and it may have been the right thing to parent them. Younger sisters generally were seen as if they were spokes of a wheel who related to each other primarily through a central hub of authority. Now that most applicants are mature men and women who have had career and family responsibilities, this kind of quasi-parenting is not appropriate. Quite the contrary: the desired goal for interaction in religious community has changed to a more weblike model, where all members relate to one another in an increasingly lateral and person-to-person way.

However, even today, developing peer relationships in community is rarely easy. It entails a slow, communal maturing, a growth from codependence reminiscent of an infant's natural reliance on parents and caregivers to a mature consciousness of self. In other words, mature love must be grown into; it is rooted in real experience, not in ideals or expectations. A community "building itself up in love" is always easier to envision than to achieve. Over the years I have found that it is very important to remember what theologian Dietrich Bonhoeffer wrote in *Life Together:* "He who loves his dream of a community more than the Christian community itself becomes a destroyer of the latter, even though his personal intentions may be ever so honest and earnest and sacrificial."[8]

I myself have often been tempted to dream that if we had a different community—different sisters, or sisters more dedicated to the ideals I cherish, younger sisters or just more of them—*then* our community would flourish. I try to remember not only Bonhoeffer's warning, but the wisdom of the former coach of the Miami Dolphins, Don Shula, "You gotta play the game with the players you got!" Every community, just as every person, must be accepted and loved *where it is,* in order to have any chance for change and transformation. If it is constantly being reminded of missing the mark, the chances are better for depression than for growth. C. S. Lewis wrote somewhere that if you pull up an acorn every two weeks to criticize it for not being an oak, you will probably never get an oak tree. None of this is to say that we should not *have* ideals, but that we must not give preference to the desired abstract at the cost of the living reality.

To love the reality of the actual community in which we find ourselves may be particularly difficult for those who helped form or lead it in past times. I have known retired religious superiors to speak with regret, and sometimes with bitterness, of how much closer to some ideal of poverty, obedience, or simplicity of life their community was decades ago—and perhaps on their watch—than at the present time. "When I was a novice, it was a big treat to have an ice cream cone, and now the brothers go out for dinner!" "In my day we had two habits and a change of underwear, and now sisters don't have enough room in their closets for their secular clothes!" In many cases such reflections state an unfortunate truth—some laxity or loss of spirit—but the accompanying bitterness is not helpful when comparisons obstruct the more important need to love the community *as it is now.*

At this point a reader may well ask, "But what, more precisely, *is* so hard and complicated about loving one another, about 'building up in love'"? It is not always easy to see how love's difficulties present themselves in the actual context of day-to-day living and minute-by-minute choice. A specific, if fictional, example may help. Let us imagine a sister called Felicia who has a great respect for the divine office, which her community chants in chapel regularly every day. Unless she is away or seriously incapacitated, she makes it a point to be in her choir stall at the appointed times. Felicia feels that the daily office is not only the "work of God" but also her job—being professed means being a professional, and chanting the psalms is a good part of what she does for her vocation and her livelihood. But another member of her community—Sister Winifred—is frail, and tires easily. She sometimes comes to chapel and sometimes not, especially at the shorter noonday and evening offices. For many months Sister Felicia holds her peace, because she cannot know at any one time how tired or ill Sister Winifred is, or how hard she tried to get to chapel. The custom of the convent is that if a sister does not feel well, the community will trust her decision for added rest.

Felicia continues for quite a while to give Winifred the benefit of the doubt. Then one evening at household recreation, Winifred relates that she was on a shopping trip that morning, and extended her time away to visit and play with a neighbor's new litter of puppies. Presumably this explains why she was not at noon prayers that day. Now Felicia is really annoyed. After several similar instances, when Winifred seems to have had energy for other things but not for chapel, Felicia's concern about the situation escalates. In praying about the matter, Felicia is forced to notice that although her own annoyance is threatening to destroy the love between herself and Winifred, the other sisters do not seem to be as put out by Winifred's behavior as she is. "Is this my problem?" Felicia asks herself. "Am I envious of Winifred's freedom because she is getting away with something I would like to do? Am I, like the older brother in the parable of the prodigal son, bitter because my faithfulness is not being noticed or rewarded? Am I resentful like the laborers in the vineyard, who at the end of a long day got no more wages than those who worked just an hour?"

Felicia ponders all this and tries to find the root of her nagging resentment. Does it, she wonders, have anything to do with the fact that as a little girl I felt that my mother overlooked in my younger brother all *his* escapades and shirking of chores, and expected *me* to be the responsible child? After a time of soul-searching Felicia decides it is so, and after she has recognized and accepted some of the cause of her resentment, she feels a little more at peace. But then she thinks: "Even if I can clear the air of my own personal resentment, is this still a matter that needs to be addressed for the good of the community? Is Winifred's seemingly casual or at least erratic approach to the work of the divine office affecting the younger women who are still in process of discernment? Is the fabric of our common worship being frayed?" Finally Felicia asks herself, "Should someone talk to Winifred about being with the community in chapel? If that is so, I know it must be done in love and for the sake of the common good. Should I be the one to speak? If I *am* the one, how and when should I do it?"

With that difficult prospect ahead of her, Felicia seeks out Sister Naomi, an elder in the community, who is known for wisdom and the ability to maintain confidentiality. Felicia speaks to Naomi about her concern as a sort of "dress rehearsal" for speaking directly to Winifred. She also comes to Naomi for a "reality check," to get an objective perspective on the situation and what she feels called to do. The bottom-line question in Felicia's mind is: Will speaking to Winifred do any good? Will it build up community or tear it down? Will it make love or war? And will she herself be heard?

At the time I was stationed in our convent in Augusta, Georgia, as a novice, I took on the role of Sister Winifred myself. The professed sisters spoke to me one day about a certain behavior that was unacceptable to the community—namely, my tendency to dominate general conversations among the sisters. I didn't understand my sisters' criticism at the time, or for many years later; I thought they meant I took up too much "air time" during discussions. So I began to ration myself to two comments per meeting, but this did not seem to satisfy anybody. Then I was sent to a workshop on relationships, and from there into therapy in order "to learn better communication skills." All this was deeply hurtful to me as I didn't really understand the problem, and I certainly didn't know what to do about it other than to avoid any contribution whatsoever to our conversations! The confrontation might easily have alienated me from community or repressed a good part of my energy and passion, but I simply persevered and tried to do what I was asked to do, and by God's grace, lost neither my vocation nor my sense of self.

Many years later I *did* understand. Always a vocal and articulate person, I had learned in graduate school to enter every conversation, argument, or debate with an "everyone for themselves" attitude. But what seemed fine in the company of highly educated and competitive peers—most of them men, many older or more forceful than I—had the opposite effect in my small household of sisters. Some of them were not accustomed to jumping right in, and needed to be given some time and space in which to craft their offerings to the conversation. This insight went along with another major truth I learned:"It is not enough to be right; it is more important to be loving."

Obstacles to healthy relationship in community can sound far more trivial than they are experienced. There is a story about Saint Thérèse of Lisieux, whose seat in choir was next to a sister who obsessively ran her rosary beads across her teeth. In time this little noise became a great irritation to Thérèse. How should she best love this sister? First, I imagine, she had to learn how to be aware and honest about her own discomfort, and then how to decide whether to choose to tolerate the annoyance, or take some action to stop it. For there is always the option of simply bearing with the annoyance. This may be a healthy choice as long as it is not the repression of feelings or capitulation out of fear; such acceptance must be truly *chosen*. Repressed feelings are like toothpaste in a tube—under enough stress a capped tube will crack open and the paste will ooze out at an inappropriate point. On the other hand, freely choosing to bear a difficult thing may be a gift of love.

I once sat next to a sister in choir who drank coffee early in the morning before Matins, so that I prayed the office smelling her coffee-laden breath. I found it unpleasant. I could have pretended the problem did not exist, or ignored it in the hope it would go away, telling myself: "The smell of coffee before Matins shouldn't, and therefore doesn't really bother me." Or I could have taken the opposite course of trying to stamp out the problem or fix it by unthinking action: "I'll put a note on her choir stall, 'Please brush your teeth after you drink early morning coffee.'" In the end I chose not to complain about it. My complaining might have turned sour one of her most cherished creature comforts. It might also sour our relationship, which had taken hard work to build up. In deciding not to say anything to her I wasn't repressing anything, but freely choosing to cope with that small inconvenience. Now, ironically, I myself drink coffee before Matins. Although sisters don't sit as close together in choir as we used to, I find myself wondering if another sister is offended by my breath and is choosing not to tell *me* out of love!

We human beings are complex creatures, and complexity is hard to live with. I once lived in a house with a sister who always greeted me with an especially big smile. Yet I happened to know that not only was she dealing with terribly painful problems, but she had also acted in ways that had hurt other people. Who was I going to respond to—the sister in pain, the sister whose actions hurt others, or the sister with the happy smile? How could I respond to and love the truth of her complex being? In asking this question I ran against the concept, attributed to Augustine of Hippo, of "hate the sin, love the sinner." In other words, accept the human being but reject those destructive behaviors that can tear down community. (What Saint Augustine actually wrote is *Cum dilectione hominum et odio vitiorum,* "with delight in humanity and hatred of vice.") However, I have never found it easy to separate out the sin from the sinner, the destructive behavior from the person herself, especially when she does not see her own actions *as* wrongdoing and, far from changing or repenting, continues to dominate and put down others. It has taken slow-growing knowledge and acceptance of my own failings to begin to see beyond the faults of my sisters to the true self within that is to be accepted and loved.

An Indian parable has helped me greatly in discerning the true self within myself and others, and loving the apparently "unlovable." At one time in India people made lamps out of camel stomachs. When cured, these membranes had the consistency of parchment and the shape of globes. They were decorated with painted designs and then a candle was inserted at the bottom so that the globe served as a lampshade. Now the point is that the candle flame was the same in every lamp, but the shade varied greatly. Some camel stomachs were very thick and heavily decorated; some were paper-thin and translucent. So it is with us human vessels. Even though the light is the same—for Christians, it is called the light of Christ—some shades, or personalities, are so thick that it is almost impossible to see the light. Other personalities seem to have a very thin shade, and through them you can see a good deal of light.

But I have had to be careful not to focus so entirely on what I try to see as the light in others that I disregard the unique reality of the lampshade. I have found in myself a fault of demanding that others should shine out with the same degree of light or in the same manner that I do. Some of the hardest inner work I have done is to try to stop placing unreal expectations on others. Before I ever came to the convent, I had a friend with whom I loved to stay up till all hours talking about the great questions of humanity such as the problem of evil and the immortality of the soul. There came a time, however, when my friend wasn't keeping up with my tireless intellectual curiosity. Wasn't, couldn't, or didn't want to? I couldn't tell. But I kept pressuring her until she no longer wanted any part of our long talks. Didn't really seem to want me as a friend anymore. It came to me that we had been walking down a road together, hand in hand, and then at some point—whether I pulled on ahead or she pulled away—our hands and our paths parted. Since then I have often recalled with some shame how I was so blinded by my own ego and intellectual drive that I could not see and respect her true, different, and lovely self.

At a later time I became aware that I had placed the same sort of unreal expectations on my sisters, and in fact on my entire community. I have noticed that many religious men and women do the same—and this tendency is not restricted to newcomers to the religious life. Many of us expect religious community to be the ideal context of love, support, holiness, and service to the needy, all of which will make those of us who live in the community feel fulfilled and worthwhile. I once held a very distorted idea of my motives for entering the convent in the first place and my reasons for staying, vaguely supposing they were "to love God and serve God's people." In reality, one of my real motives for coming was the desire to prove somehow that the consumerist values of my parents were despicable. The moment of truth came soon after my mother died. I was in the room with her when the nurse said, "Sister, your mother has expired." After saying some prayers I picked up the room phone, and, in a rather shaky voice, I called my psychiatrist. Two days later I went to my next session. The first thing he said to me was, "Well, now that your mother has died, and your reason for being in the convent no longer exists, what are you going to do with the rest of your life?" Of course my first reaction was fury—how could he be so crude, cruel, and unfeeling? But almost immediately I saw my two alternatives: to storm out in rage, or to hang on a minute and consider what he had said. I stayed. I considered. His remark eventually cut away some of the blind spots in my vision of my vocation—the need to prove my values right and my mother's wrong. That insight was an important milestone in my journey to clarity and freedom, a big step toward my acceptance of the Order of Saint Helena as simply itself, and myself as myself.

Before I came to community and for many years as a young monastic, I thought I knew not only why I had come to community, but what religious life was all about. Only slowly over the decades did I begin to understand what this life together and apart really is about. In his classic book *Asylums,* Erving Goffman discusses the "closed community," among which he includes mental institutions, prisons, army training camps, naval vessels, nursing homes—and convents and monasteries! The inclusion of monastic houses in this list at first seemed strange, but on further thought, organizational similarities exist. If I remember "the bad old days" of traditional religious life, the comparisons may evoke a wry smile. A religious community living closely together can, without sufficient discernment, attention, and care, sometimes engender feelings of being trapped, not unlike those in other closed communities. I knew of a convent where there was a superior who had no liking for one novice whom she seemed constantly to criticize, put down, and discount. On the other hand, the same superior had great affection for a pet dog who followed her everywhere—even to chapel and refectory. The young woman could not stand up for herself in these hurtful circumstances, and that made her feel less valued than the dog. Partly because there was no recourse for speaking or writing to anyone outside the community about such a hurtful injustice, it was easy for the young novice to feel imprisoned and to want to escape.

Someone once said of the cloister that it does not automatically ensure holiness: a wall may enclose a lovely secret garden, or a stinking rubbish heap. I have found in convents and monasteries climates that may range from deeply safe and holy to intensely unsafe and even demonic. In my experience this heightening of a healthy or a toxic environment can be found even in monastic houses that are not enclosed in a strict sense; where the members go out for ministry and guests come in for hospitality.

The apparent safety and stability of religious life can be deceiving. More than one parish priest has called the convent to refer a woman too unstable or too frail emotionally to make it in everyday life, but whom her rector thought might "survive" in a convent—as if life and relationship in religious community is easier than life "outside." Although in a community dedicated to Christ there may be found true comfort and deep joy, the religious life does not exist for our protection. At its best community life is one of mutual support, but it should never be seen as a surrogate parent to supply the affirmation and nurture we never had in our own families.

A branch house of ours once included a sister who was not yet life professed and who eventually found her vocation elsewhere. While she was with us, she often seemed so very angry and aggressive that some of us became wary of entering the same room with her. We felt as if our angry sister was swinging an ax up and down, and we had to be careful to cross the room quickly before the ax fell again! Such active aggression in a household can create a toxic atmosphere, where community withers and is displaced by fear. Unfortunately, *passive* aggression can produce just as toxic an atmosphere. At one early point in the development of that same household, I noticed that one day the compost pot would be above the sink in the kitchen and a day later it would be put under the sink. Then a day or two later it would reappear back over the sink. Obviously one sister thought it would be better kept in one place and another disagreed. But nobody, so far as I knew, talked about this; nobody said *why* it would be better one place or the other. Fairly soon the moving of the compost pot felt like a contest, a hostile act. Instances such as these have to be faced, named, and lived through, and in some cases personnel changes need to occur before the toxic atmosphere can modulate into one of trust.

The health of a community is to some degree the aggregate of the psychic and spiritual health of its members. Any ongoing group of people contains a wide range of mental and emotional health, from very stable and healthy persons to others who are mentally and emotionally compromised. I once heard of a very interesting speculation that was given by a Jesuit superior general. It was reported that he drew a vertical oval, an upended egg shape, and divided it into three major segments, labeling them from the top: 20 percent, 60 percent, and 20 percent. He said that in his visitations he had observed that on a rough average the top 20 percent of any given religious community were individuated persons who would continue to grow and flourish no matter where they were. He said that the bottom 20 percent were individuals so severely emotionally or psychologically compromised that they would probably deteriorate over the years no matter in what context they lived. Then he further drew a dotted line horizontally bisecting the middle 60 percent. The lower half of the 60 percent seemed to him to flourish and grow in religious community with the help of psychotherapy; the upper 30 percent would grow and thrive simply because of living in a supportive community. He said further that he had observed the disturbing fact that in many of the communities he visited, most of the emotional and financial resources were spent on the bottom 20 percent, where they might have the least effect for growth or change. This may well be true, but I also try to remember that *wholeness* is not entirely synonymous with *holiness*. I have known individuals who were quite emotionally and mentally healthy but who could not, even in charity, be called holy; I have also known persons who were not so very emotionally or psychically mature but whose spirituality and relationship with God were rock solid and full of holy wisdom.

Given the wide range of personalities in any community, the question remains: "How do we love the unlovable?" How can we relate lovingly not only to those who have a capacity for returning our love, but to those capable only of self-survival behaviors that may have the effect of annoying, hurting, or betraying us? I believe that there is no single satisfactory answer; instead, here is a parable. At one time I studied drama. I was in an acting class where a young woman complained that she couldn't honestly play a certain love scene because she didn't love the man who was cast as her opposite. Hers was essentially our question: how do you behave lovingly to the unlovable without hypocrisy? The instructor answered her: "Well, find just one thing about him that you honestly find attractive. Perhaps it is his earlobe. Then play the scene to that earlobe." For us the "earlobe" may be the true person before us, not the presenting persona and its motives, actions, or defenses. Our "earlobe" ultimately is the candle flame in the Indian lantern, the light of divine consciousness within each person. However, having intended love to that core being of an individual, real or "tough" love may require us not to enable them, perhaps to confront them or not to vote for them, perhaps to separate them from community, or as a last resort to put them in a safe place where they can no longer hurt themselves or others.

An unsafe or toxic atmosphere in religious community, a place that is assumed to be one of support and healing, can be hard to recognize or even speak about. Far too often an oppressive situation, if it is not totally repressed, is ignored; it becomes the proverbial "elephant in the middle of the living room," by which everyone is negatively affected but to which no one refers. This kind of dishonesty breeds fear; it is only truth that leads to freedom. So the first step to health in community is the awareness of an unhealthy situation. Even this initial awareness is not as easy as it may sound. Awareness takes attention and practice. The Zen injunction, "Wake up!

Be there!" is a prod to attentiveness, and perhaps Saint Paul's "pray unceasingly" is the Christian version. After awareness the next step is shared discussion and then, finally, discernment and execution of the appropriate action. I am grateful to live in a community that is fairly adept at knowing that there is an elephant in the living room. I think it is fair to say that most of the time we are even able to name it and discuss it. What is much harder is managing to get the elephant *out* of the living room. The alternative to the violent expulsion of a community member, which can be justified only in extreme cases, is confrontation, reconciliation, or, if necessary, a carefully considered and loving separation.

Stress and tension in a religious house are often elements that make for an unsafe atmosphere, but not always. When a group works hard to find and honor its truth, the pain of tension and stress can be more like labor pains than death throes. Our Sister Catherine Josephine used to have a rock polisher, and from using it she came up with a metaphor to describe community: as we rub up against one another like the rocks in the tumbler, we may either become worn away, or become smoother and lovelier. How we emerge from the polisher depends on a number of factors, such as the condition of the "rock" before the polishing began and the degree of abrasiveness in the process. Much of the discernment on the part of an aspirant to the religious life lies in this question: Will the intensity of this life be enhancing or erosive? Will I be strengthened or diminished?

It is difficult to describe, though not so difficult to feel, when a stressful situation crosses an invisible line to become a damaging one. Stress, and even conflict, can be raw material for growth and wisdom, but they can also cause damage. Of course the same stressful situation may challenge and strengthen one person while it emotionally damages another. One of the hardest lessons I've had to learn in community relationship is to avoid this thought: "If *I* can cope with it, and grow through it, *everyone* should be able to." On the contrary, as Saint Paul wrote to the Christians in Corinth who were lording it over their "unspiritual" brothers and sisters, "To the weak I became weak, so that I might win the weak" (1 Corinthians 9:22). I think Paul means that when he was with Christians weaker than he was, he related to them not out of his strength, but out of his own weakness. In other words, he discovered the reality of his own powerlessness, even his own sin, and from that place of reality within himself he met the weakness of others. Where we *are* is our truth, not where we think we ought to be. Where we are is where God meets us, and that is the true humility that will make us free. Accepting the truth of our vulnerability is hard—first it may make us miserable, but *then* it will make us free!

Some of the stress that arises in community life comes from insecurity trying to clothe itself as power. A weak person may try to make another lesser, so that she or he may feel stronger. This unfortunate dynamic can manifest itself in an individual, or in a sort of *folie á deux*. What used to be called "particular friendships" in religious community most often had little or nothing to do with misplaced sexuality—which was so often feared or implied—and more to do with two persons who felt themselves weak, trying to bolster up their self-images by criticizing others, particularly perhaps authority, and generally creating disharmony. Many visitors to our convent have said that they can sense whether a religious community is living in either harmony or conflict, that you can tell by subtle things such as the way choir sounds when the community antiphonally chants the psalms. In times of stress or conflict, it can seem that the two sides of choir are competing or challenging one another in volume or pace. Living so closely together, it is important to maintain a stress-free daily rhythm and an atmosphere of mutual respect.

Often fair and efficient leadership, whether designated or undesignated, is the "oil" that keeps the "machinery" of relationships and daily life moving along smoothly. As life together in community has evolved over the decades, styles of leadership have changed dramatically. A great deal of attention has been paid to what it means to be in authority, to govern and to be governed in Christian community. What does it mean to be a branch of the vine and a member of the body of which Christ is sum and head? What does it mean to be both leader and one who is led in the context of religious life?

Some years ago I had a splendid experience of collegial religious leadership while on mission for four months in Canada as part of a campus ministry team. There were eight of us living together in a small house on the campus. Although most of the time we were a community of peers, when a difficult situation arose, or when a hard decision had to be made, the monk who was the head of our team ministry, David Hemming, SSJE, either took that responsibility on himself or made sure someone else did. His leadership was almost invisible. David had a gift for seeing the overall picture and making things happen for the good of all, but those gifts were not more valued in our house than those of the sister who prepared our meals, the gifts of the campus ministry team, or those of the brothers who were taking classes. One particular incident made me very much aware of our interdependence. David was invited to a performance and special dinner in his honor by the choir of Kings College, Cambridge, which happened to be on a Canadian tour. (He had sung in that choir when he was at university.) When we heard about his invitation, we insisted he get spruced up for the occasion— one of the brothers lent him a tie, one of us shined up his shoes, and I remember it was my job to sew a couple of brass buttons on his blazer! I have always remembered that day as a perfect example of the mutual gift so important in religious community. The whole experience taught me early on that a hierarchical or "top-down" style of relating was contrary to the Christian model whereby each member of the body is equally valued and necessary to its healthy functioning.

"Almost invisible" leadership is generally leadership ready to work itself out of a job, so that each person in a group may relate to one another directly without always going through a superior. Currently all of our houses function with no one sister in charge; various sisters oversee areas such as library, guests, bursary, maintenance, sacristy, grounds, and kitchen. Decisions that affect the whole household may be brought to the group's attention by any member, and are made in weekly house meetings. The assembled household tries to come to a common mind and decide by consensus, or occasionally, if necessary, by informal vote.

The house meeting evolved from ancient monastic chapter meetings—held daily, weekly, and/or annually— where an abbot or abbess would gather the community to listen to the brothers or sisters, and give instructions and guidance for the common good. In our convents the sisters take turns in chairing the weekly meetings.

One of the things that I find most helpful in relating well with my sisters is the way we begin these meetings in the convent where I now live. We have a few moments of silence and then one of us—anyone who feels called—offers a brief prayer, sometimes as brief as "Amen." Then each sister, in no particular order, "checks in." This checking-in is to let the others know as much or as little as each wants to share about what has happened during the past week and what is going on for her now. To give an instance, this is more or less what I found myself saying at a recent meeting: "I'm really grateful for the miracles of modern medicine—my back has been doing wonderfully well this week. I'm also feeling so glad that my brother is fully recovered from his surgery and is able to travel again to do lectures in far off places on the new research he's been involved with. Thanks so much for your prayers! I do find that I have some concern—well, anxiety—about our upcoming Annual Chapter meetings, but then I always do, and things always seem to come together."

In the very early days of Christianity there seemed to have been a similar form of governance. Leaders were raised up from local communities who encouraged mutual participation and interdependence. We can read of some of this in the book of Acts. Western monasticism might well claim as its heritage not only the desert, but also the beginnings of communities in the cities, *koinonia,* where members were connected to one another in the love of Christ. The early Christian community in Jerusalem was described as holding all things in common, and joining together in common prayer. Saint Paul, writing to another such group of disciples, gives us a striking metaphor of leadership when he calls Christ "the head of the body, the church" (Colossians 1:18). The head needs the body as much as the body needs the head and all members must work together in mutual cooperation.

Good leadership, besides moving toward the goal of collegiality, encourages and helps to create a safe and healthy atmosphere. What is a healthy atmosphere? I believe community welfare is an accretion of quite small things, such as the proverbial "random acts of kindness." I knew of a monastery, for example, where the prior established the practice of giving a "Brother of the Week" award. The monk who had received the award for that week would give the award on the following week. The award honored small acts of generosity or kindness such as dealing with an emotionally unstable drop-in, vacuuming the interiors of the cars (which was no one's particular assignment), or voluntarily picking up the jobs of a brother who was called away for a family emergency. At first such a practice of award-giving might seem childish, but it had the effect of encouraging the brothers to notice and affirm each other's attempts to build up the community in generosity and love.

I once lived in a branch house with three other sisters. We had no titular leader, but each one of us took our share of responsibility for the household's welfare. Two of us were "morning people": we went to our rooms right after Compline—the last prayer service of the day—and were up for meditation and reading or writing at least two hours before Matins in chapel the next day. The other two sisters were "night people": they stayed up reading the newspaper or working or praying in the evening and slept till the last possible minute in the morning. In that milieu both of these preferences were respected and supported; and in general the strange ways and preferences of others were celebrated rather than criticized or laughed at. This kind of safety partly consists in our simply being there for one another, and seeing their otherness as interesting rather than something of which to be fearful or critical.

It is easier to foster smooth relationships if the people living together are aware of each other's essential needs. In another household I was once in, the sister in charge arranged a meeting as we began the convent year to ask each other to share what each personally needed for well-being of body and spirit. I was grateful to be able to speak my needs to my sisters and to hear theirs. I remember that on my list were such things as membership in the local "Y" so that I could swim laps regularly, and an agreement not to do business after Compline so that I could get to bed early and have the silent morning hours before Matins for contemplation and writing. Most of us had received our household's consent to do these things already, so the benefit of our listening to one another was not so much a matter of getting permission as of receiving confirmation and support.

Leadership styles can range from very hierarchical and structured to so "laid back" that chaos can result. A third alternative is a more consensual and collegial style. I have known of communities that have supported each of these ways of living together. Sometimes a more structured and formal style can have its advantages. I have noticed that novices who are struggling with their own inner and outer transitional chaos are often more drawn to the formal and ritual aspects of the life, such as the habit and the regularity of the traditional schedule, than the "old hands" who have moved through transition to an easier and more flexible way of being. It sometimes happens that a firm and regularized leadership style is necessary to stabilize a community before it can move into the risk of openness to experimentation. More structured and conservative religious communities may offer safety and security to individuals in spiritual distress, and to groups of persons in times of cultural chaos. Such institutions, however, do not readily foster personal growth and freedom and they can become constricting or oppressive.

My own earliest experience of authority in religious community was, as I have said, at best a bit skewed, and at worst downright unhealthy. But in some ways I think by God's grace I received what I needed. I was coming out of a very chaotic and transitional period in my own life—the five years of my conversion and then the painful marriage and divorce—and in a way the hierarchical structure of my first community was stabilizing. At that point it seemed freeing *not* to have to make any more decisions for myself. The oppressive aspect of hierarchical leadership surfaced soon enough, however, and at the end of my time there I had come to the stage in my spiritual and emotional journey where I was ready in a new way to begin the move toward personal choice and responsibility.

My present community initiated its movement toward self-awareness and renewal in the 1960s and early 70s. Our challenge was to keep what was valuable in our formularies and tradition and to abandon only what was repressive or no longer useful, but this involved a certain amount of trial and error. For example, along with almost everything else we questioned the value of the Great Silence, which traditionally extends from after Compline—the closing service of the day—until after morning prayers and Eucharist. We tried dispensing with all periods of silence. But after only a few days of sisters talking to one another before morning prayers, we realized that living so closely we needed the silence if we were not to bite each others' heads off at breakfast! We learned that for us the silence was not an outmoded convention, but a treasured and integral part of our life.

In another case we learned the hard way that even the most desired outcome is much better chosen than imposed. When I entered community it was assumed that nuns didn't smoke—if a sister lit up a cigarette, she would immediately self-destruct! But we also noticed that at conferences on the religious life, the *monks* would gather outside to smoke and chat together, and, far from self-destructing, they seemed to have much more fun! Was this disparity between monks and nuns a question of poverty, holiness, or outdated male chauvinism? Consequently, those of us who had smoked before we came to community, some of whom had not had a cigarette for decades, started smoking again. Eventually we all stopped, not because "nuns don't smoke," but for the same reasons other people do—we chose to. The whole process of renewal was an exercise in communal questioning that led us out of the constriction (and safety) of formalism, and pointed the community and its members toward a regime of personal responsibility and choice. This was only the beginning of our review of the way we live; the process of renewal continues today.

The questioning and upheaval that can accompany such change has, of course, some less fortunate side effects. For instance, when we moved away from wearing the traditional habit all the time, we ran the risk of looking—particularly in chapel—a bit like a group of what my mother called "raggle-taggle gypsies." Many sisters did not know how to dress well in contemporary and becoming clothes, and those of us who thought we did were limited by what came to us secondhand from friends, associates, or the local thrift shop. Furthermore, the move beyond formalism is not only sometimes unedifying, but it can be regrettable. There is always the possibility of "throwing out the baby with the bathwater." Fortunately, we did not completely forsake the habit, but now wear it as a liturgical garment on appropriate occasions. Now I sometimes think of my traditional habit as the clothing of my profession, useful for identification in the way a flight attendant may be recognized by his or her clothing, or as a priest puts on a stole to celebrate the Eucharist. In a way my habit is my "work clothes."

Renewal and change may be especially challenging to those in positions of authority. One of our former superiors, toward the beginning of our renewal process, said that when she was feeling pressured she still made decisions by fiat. Only when she felt grounded and at peace with herself could she listen to all sides and exercise the authority that enables the forming of the common mind. "Authority" is an interesting word; it carries in its root meaning a significant distinction from ruling by fiat and domination: *auctoritas* comes from the Latin *augeo,* meaning to cause to increase, to lead to fulfillment. From *augeo* we derive the word "augment"; true authority enhances and increases, rather than suppresses, those for whom it is responsible. I once ran across a wonderful example of true authority in the writings of T. S. Eliot, who claimed that the theologian and novelist Charles Williams had true authority because, instead of making people feel awkward or insignificant in his presence, people invariably felt themselves to be more intelligent and more valued than ever before.

When authority listens carefully to the needs and insights of its constituency, it is taking the first big step toward collegiality. Saint Benedict put a high value on obedience to the abbot, but he also understood that obedience, listening with the "ear of the heart," applied not only to the brethren who gave their obedience, but to the abbot who received it. Benedict writes in chapter 3 of his Rule:

> Whenever any important business is to be done in the monastery, let the abbot call together the whole community and state the matter to be acted upon. Then, having heard the Brethren's advice, let him turn the matter over in his mind and do what he shall judge to be most expedient. The reason we have said that all should be called for counsel is that the Lord often reveals to the youngest what is best.[9]

If decision-making by all concerned is the preferred method, however, a natural question arises: Why have any leadership at all? Perhaps the answer is that nature abhors a vacuum, and without a designated leader, ambitious and sometimes self-serving persons will hasten to fill the void. This is only one example of why the transition from hierarchical leadership to communal leadership is not only a hard road, but a bumpy one. The purpose of autocratic leadership may be to "self-destruct," in favor of consensus, but careful discernment is crucial as to whom and at what point to hand over control. The change cannot be accomplished by fiat—the leader must retain the responsibility until the conditions are right for others to assume it. Premature abdication, as in the case of King Lear, only ushers in conflict and chaos. The same warning can apply to unthinking delegation; if tasks and roles are doled out indiscriminately, the work will not be well done. Good delegation is the opposite of "dumping" responsibilities. A leader who is skilled at delegating discerns not only who can do a particular job, but who will find in it a source of challenge leading eventually to satisfaction.

Despite these and similar difficulties, shared leadership and governance by consensus are not only more beneficial to the body but also more effective in the long run. When each member has contributed to a project or discussion, and has felt that his or her position has been valued and heard, each can claim a share in the final outcome. People have ownership in what they have helped create, and are far less likely to undermine or sabotage the decision or project later.

One model in religious community for moving from hierarchical leadership is leadership by an elected council. A major advantage of a council is that it diffuses the mystique of leadership and discourages unrealistic projections. Such projections may be of a positive or a negative kind. Both superiors and bosses naturally accrue to themselves parental projections of both the filler of needs and also the threat to individuality. A council diffuses these projections—it is harder to make several people into a parent-figure than one alone. A council may still become the focus of misdirected blame and resentment for members' needs that, rightly or wrongly, are felt not to be met, but it tends to be to a lesser extent than a single leader. Another challenge to governing by a council arises when, in a pressing situation, no one person has ultimate authority for resolving it; each member of a team may assume that the responsibility lies with someone else and so things may occasionally "fall through the cracks."

But despite the challenges of shared leadership, it has two further significant advantages. First, it shares the burden of responsibility so that each member of the team can have some freedom to pursue other interests and ministry. Second, there is less danger that the role will become confused with one's identity. Being the sole leader may not only consume all one's time and energies, but it may distract one's soul from its rightful perspective. Perhaps for this reason many of the church's greatest leaders, including Benedict and Gregory the Great, fled from authority until circumstances and their consciences would allow them to flee no more. Besides the "daily pressure" of what Saint Paul called his "anxiety for all the churches" (2 Corinthians 11:28), there is the profound spiritual reason to flee leadership. Even though it is truly a trade or skill among all other trades or skills, most people do not see it that way. Leadership is generally associated with glamour and prestige. Success can be a great spiritual danger; it attracts both positive and negative projections like a magnet attracts iron filings. The leader in religious community—abbot, abbess, prior, prioress, reverend father, mother, guardian, or superior—is in a very high profile position indeed. The temptation for someone in any of those roles is to take on the projections, becoming a persona rather than a person—a creation in the image of glamour rather than a creature in the image of God. This risk pertains even to big frogs in quite small ponds. Perhaps the lure of power begins in the privilege and power that children associate with their parents. I have known a religious superior who, when she was in office, administered well and gracefully, but when she stepped down, she became depressed and bitter. She seemed not to know how to relate to those whom she once governed—they no longer related to her with the same deference and affection—and even not to know who she was herself anymore.

As a novice I was told by an elderly sister that I was destined for leadership in the community. I found myself praying that I should not be given high-profile authority until I truly did not desire it, until I did not need it to feel myself affirmed or valued. God gave me the grace to intuit the danger such a position might present to my needy psyche. God also gave me the grace of enough time—perhaps *just* enough time—before I was tapped for major responsibility. When I did find myself in a long series of positions of responsibility and authority, I continued to pay serious attention to keeping my identity and my role separate, and to take steps to keep my spirit and self-image in touch with reality.

Another danger of leadership, especially leadership by one person, is the uncertainty, or fickleness, of human nature. Down through the ages, too often a group will call a person with leadership qualities to rectify and order a chaotic situation for them, and then, if the person uncovers and confronts uncomfortable truths, the group will turn and try to trivialize, marginalize, or rid themselves of the reformer, the "gadfly." We do not know exactly how Saint Benedict received his call to the religious life, but presumably he knew his gifts for potential leadership and was also aware of some of the risks that accompany it. Benedict left Rome and Roman society. He took with him only the man who had been his guardian or "nurse" in his childhood, and went to live in a cave for three years in the Simbrucini Mountains about forty miles from Rome, obtaining food from a monk whom he befriended whose monastery was on the mountain above the cave. In solitude and the sound of sheer silence Benedict listened and responded to his vocation. After the three years his solitude was interrupted by the monks of a nearby monastery, who begged him to become their abbot. He was reluctant to accept, but finally did, and set about to correct the abuses of the monastery. This was more than the monks had bargained for. One day, we are told, they presented Benedict with a glass of poisoned wine. When he made the sign of the cross over it, the glass shattered. But realizing that his brothers wished him out of the way, Benedict returned to his cave. What is so poignant here is not so much the myth of miraculous powers, but the very human truth of the story. Benedict's life gives us a vivid example of the possible cost involved in the call to monastic discipleship and leadership.

With these considerations it is no wonder that a leader often feels lonely. But perhaps *every* individual in religious community at some time experiences loneliness. There is for the monastic no *human* significant other to whom at the end of the day one can turn for comfort and warmth. Without that particular human commitment it is hard to feel understood and companioned. There is a hunger for another human being to be on the same path, to journey together and to fill the loneliness. For all people there are two major forms of loneliness: neurotic loneliness and existential loneliness. In my case, for instance, my neurotic loneliness probably had a lot to do with my father's death when I was a child, my mother's incapacity for expressions of affection, and my unconscious wish for the religious community to supply those needs.

My own path has been to move very slowly beyond neurotic loneliness toward existential loneliness. Loneliness is existential when it realizes that no human being, or group of human beings—even, or perhaps especially, religious community—can fully meet one's need to be loved and affirmed. Only God knows the depths of both my ugliness and my beauty, my need and my gifts. One of the great blessings of the religious life is the vow made to God in the midst of a community of people who are intending to relate to God as their "significant other." In the strength and confidence (most of the time!) of that primary vowing of one's own spirit to the Holy Spirit, it is possible to grow in the hard work of loving oneself and one's brothers and sisters more and more cleanly and maturely. The corollary to accepting existential loneliness is continuing attention to healthy and healing human relationship.

In the end, what makes a community of healthy relationships? I would say healthy relationships in community are founded in reality, in what is really going on between people. Discerning relational truth takes attention and courage, because the reality is often hidden, repressed, or far less than ideal. When, and to the extent that truth is discerned, health comes from trying to act and speak in that truth as allies rather than adversaries. Finally, healthy and holy relationships are a by-product of striving for understanding, patience, welcome, and negotiation, even if those qualities may not be the most readily accessible in one's repertoire of responses.

All that is hard work. When our order was in the early stages of self-study and renewal, our superior said in jest that she was going to write a book about the life called *The Grunge and the Glory.* Living a life that is both culturally apart and intensely together is exacting. There is a lot of grunge. Life in a religious community that is committed to transformation brings an increased awareness of who one is and what is actually going on. A raised consciousness of present reality, with all its light and shadow, grunge as well as glory, increases our vulnerability—the capacity to be wounded (from Latin *vulnerare,* to wound). Sensitive people hurt one another, especially people who live, work, and pray together. As the psalmist wrote, "It is not enemies who taunt me—I could bear that; it is not adversaries who deal insolently with me—I could hide from them. But it is you, my equal, my companion, my familiar friend, with whom I kept pleasant company; we walked in the house of God with the throng" (Psalm 55:12–14). Often the injuries we experience in the present are intensified by their recalling and reopening wounds of the past. Flawed human relationship is, perhaps, the worst of the "grunge" of life in community. But the purpose of acknowledging and bearing the pain that comes our way through relationship with others is growth into wisdom and freedom—the glory of human community fully alive. The goal is to grow into the image of God—to be able to love well, choose well, act well, and become a community that strives, as in a flawed mirror, to reflect the generous freedom and love of the Holy Trinity.

+

CHAPTER FIVE

The Mixed Life: Prayer, Ministry, and Balance

For members of religious communities, as for all Christians, spiritual maturity lies in the difficult but crucial integration of being and doing, contemplation and action. A simple mandala or diagram of the mixed life as it is traditionally ordered illustrates one way this integration is lived out. It is a series of concentric circles with the daily offering of the Eucharist at the center. The Eucharist in turn is encircled by the round of praise known as the daily office, which in our community consists of Matins, Noon Prayers, Vespers, and Compline. The next concentric circle is the ministry of hospitality—inviting others in to join us in our prayer and our welcoming space, whether for an hour or a week. The next circle describes the ministries we do as individuals within the religious houses: spiritual direction, retreats, quiet days, psychotherapy, writing, art, and more. The outermost circle describes ministry outside the convent or monastery: preaching, teaching, consultation, and ministry in areas as diverse as parishes, prisons, hospitals, slums, disaster areas, and youth camps. Intersecting all of these circles are prayer and community—forming a cross: the love of God, and of self and neighbor.

Although I now see my prayer and my ministry in a profound sense as interchangeable, I can reflect on those strands in my life separately. My prayer has from the beginning been open to and formed by other spiritual traditions. I had an interesting conversation with a Zen Buddhist teacher once about the differences between our two paths of spirituality. It seemed to us that unlike Zen, my Christian faith didn't have a regularized *practice*. When students go to a Zen teacher and ask how to pray, they are told something like, "Sit on your *zafu* cushion, straighten your spine, put your active hand under the other, palms up and thumbs touching, focus your eyes on the floor about four feet in front of you, and count your breaths. When you can count your breaths up to ten without becoming distracted, watch your thoughts. Then come to *dokusan* [conference] with me next week and I will give you a *koan* to meditate on." When, on the other hand, someone comes to ask me how to pray, I have a handful of different ways to recommend but no one generally accepted practice. We realized that what my faith has that Zen doesn't is the belief that the universal Spirit is personal, and that there can be a relationship between us.

There are obvious differences between ways of prayer, but there are also surprising similarities. I was once at a conference on spirituality where we were asked to pair up with one other person and share our meditation practices. I was paired with a Zen Buddhist, this one from the Rinzai lineage—one of the more exacting forms of Japanese Zen. In our little breakout room there was a blackboard. My Buddhist friend went first. He drew a circle and quartered it. The first quarter he chalked in completely, the second quarter he left blank; in the third he drew a seated figure and in the fourth a pair of feet. He said this signified the four modes of his meditation practice, "All, nothing, Buddha mind, and extending oneself to help others." I looked at the diagram and said, "My goodness! I, as a Christian, can use that diagram too: the kataphatic way of prayer—the way of images; the apophatic way—the way of no images; the mind of Christ; and the way of ministry."

My journey in specifically Christian prayer began shortly after I was baptized in my late twenties. My spiritual director sent me back to the United States with instructions to pray for twenty minutes every day—a long time for a beginner! But I tried. I would scrupulously kneel in front of a big chair and put my arms on the seat and rest my head on my arms. As for content, I was to say the Lord's Prayer, then what I came to call my "God blesses" to hold the people I loved before God, and then to be quiet and listen. Naturally, at this point I often fell asleep. If I fell asleep *inadvertently* I would "count" it as having tried to say my prayers, but I tried conscientiously not to let this happen. For years it seemed like a fruitless practice. Then at about the fifth year of my trying and failing and trying again to pray daily in this way, something clicked. I began to feel God's presence with me when I came into the space and time of prayer. One day an allegory came to me. Suppose I had a friend and we had an agreement to meet, say, every Friday after work for a cup of coffee. It would not really matter what we talked about or how we felt about any given meeting. I could be very eager to meet one week and another week I might feel so tired I just dreaded getting myself to the meeting place. Sometimes I would have lots to tell my friend and sometimes I'd know it would be my turn to listen. But the big point is—at the end of five years we would really know one another! Something like this happened between my spirit and the Holy Spirit. I learned how to tell God (and myself) what was really going on for me, and I learned to listen for the Spirit's wisdom. So that has been my personal practice.

In prayer there is always the interaction of my human spirit and the Holy Spirit, and the interaction is one of love and intimacy. In the early days of my monastic journey, I was extremely jealous of this intimate time of being alone with God. Novices were told to take two half-hours for prayer, one in the chapel before Matins in the morning, and one in the late afternoon before Vespers. I remember that if someone came into the chapel during "my" time of early morning prayer—perhaps to set up the vessels for the Eucharist—I felt invaded and annoyed. "My" time of "private" prayer should be inviolate! It seemed to me that there was a huge gulf fixed between my personal prayer and the "common prayer" of the Eucharist and the daily office, but over the years that gap has filled in. Now it seems that both ways of praying complement and flow into one another. Moving from one to the other now is more like focusing my eyes to see up close or at a distance, and I am hardly aware of the adjustment. Perhaps in God's reality there is no such thing as "private prayer," there is only each member of the body praying within and for the well-being of the whole.

So that is how I learned to pray, but keeping my footing in a life of both intense prayer and intense activity is something else entirely! How individuals and communities live out their ways of prayer and ways of service is a matter of balance, and I, for one, have not always found that balance an easy one to achieve. For example, I have been on missions to parishes that have been so crammed with activity that although I was talking about prayer, I had no time for prayer myself, nor even the space to "hear myself think." Retreat and conference schedules can be so demanding that at times I've made myself drink lots of water so that I had a good excuse to repair to the ladies' room—the only place that no one could get at me for several minutes! That little washroom cubicle became my sanctuary. I used those precious few minutes alone in the bathroom for contemplation: how was I feeling? What did I need? How was I going to get that need met? And then I would offer a little prayer of surrender to God and a plea for God's peace, which does indeed pass understanding. Then I splashed water on my face and went back to work. That is an extreme example of ministry leaving practically no time for prayer, but I have struggled with the issue of the balance of prayer and service for most of my life as a nun.

Sometimes the balance of prayer and activity is just as hard at home, in the daily life of the convent, as it is out on mission. At one time I was asked by my community to be the sister in charge of our largest convent and also to be the novitiate director—the sister responsible for the incorporation of new members. I remember particularly one day when I was in the kitchen preparing a meal. I had a young woman assisting me who was inquiring about joining our order—while she and I peeled carrots I answered her questions. But I was also preoccupied with a phone call I needed to make after Vespers, and the letter I had to get into tomorrow morning's mail. As this kind of multitasking went on for months, I became aware that I wasn't taking my half-hours for prayer, and I felt terrible about it. When I had a chance to talk to the Holy Cross monk who was at that time our superior, it all came out: "I know that with all this responsibility, and everything I need to do, I should be praying *more,* not less, and I'm not even getting up for the prayer time before Matins!" Father Taylor looked at me with tremendous compassion in his eyes and simply said, "Oh, Sister!" Those words and that look said to me that for this particular time in my life I just needed to do the next thing that had to be done. And that, for the time being, the *yearning* to pray, to be with God, *was* my prayer.

The balance of prayer and ministry is not only the concern of individual sisters, but also a question of the ethos of communities. Although every community has some form of prayer and some form of witness or ministry, there is a broad spectrum in religious organizations. They range from an enclosed order focused almost exclusively on prayer and intercession, like the Franciscan order to which I first belonged, all the way to an active or "apostolic" community whose ministry is focused almost entirely on works and mission outside the monastery or convent, such as running schools or programs for the needy. One way to see differences lies in how many offices are said or chanted over the course of a day. The daily office is primarily a recitation, in rotation, of the psalms of David accompanied by scripture readings, hymns, and canticles. Originally seven "day" offices were recited—Lauds, Prime, Terce, Sext, Nones, Vespers, and Compline. (Matins was traditionally the night office, prayed in the early hours of the morning.) This practice has its roots in Saint Paul's injunction in 1 Thessalonians 5:17 to "pray without ceasing," and the word "office" itself comes from the Latin *officium,* meaning "obligation." The eightfold office draws its scriptural justification from Psalm 119:62 ("At midnight I rise to praise you") and 119:164 ("Seven times a day I praise you"). In our order we keep this venerable tradition because it is an ancient mode of ordering the monastic day, and its practice draws and sustains many faithful people in our own times, both monastic and lay.

A community with a more contemplative emphasis than ours would say more of the daily office, do less outside the community, and probably have a cottage industry to support itself. I know of enclosed communities that make and sell a product such as wine, cheese, bread, liqueur, or fruitcake, or offer a service such as printing books, raising dogs, creating webpages, or writing icons. A community more focused on the life of active ministry usually says fewer offices, perhaps only the greater ones of Matins and Vespers, known to Anglicans as Morning and Evening Prayer. It has fewer programs in the monastery itself, focusing instead on outreach and ministry in and to the larger community, such as work in schools, hospitals, social services, homeless shelters, and foreign mission.

Most Anglican communities combine something of these two visions in a way traditionally called "the mixed life." My own community is an example of the mixed life, and as a rule we say four of the daily offices. In the convent we hold retreats and programs, offer spiritual direction, and write books and icons. We encourage each sister to have an outside ministry for some hours or days each week—we have sisters who do hospital chaplaincy work, psychotherapy, Christian education, and work with the homeless. With the whole question of ordained ministry we are in slightly different territory, one that not so long ago was a new frontier for women. Male priests have always made a distinction between "secular" clergy (under a diocesan bishop) and "regular" clergy (under monastic "rule"). Women have just begun to explore what this means for us. One of our sisters, Mary Michael Simpson, was the first woman religious to be ordained; we now have six sister priests in our small order, and another in seminary. In the future we expect to articulate ever more clearly what it means for ordained as well as lay women to live the threefold vow in community; to grow in love, prayer, and ministry. Our sister priests do Sunday supply work or have part-time jobs in parishes, and these are only some of the many opportunities for ministry both inside and outside our convents.

Within the broad ethos of our order I have had to work out my own balance of prayer and active service. Besides the daily balance there are also periods in my life when I have felt called more toward outreach ministry or toward prayer. Because we do live in community, however, we don't make these decisions unilaterally, though as I have pointed out we increasingly negotiate and decide consensually. Of course, in "the bad old days" decisions about individual lifestyle—we call it "vocation within the vocation"—were made by fiat and were more limited in scope. I remember that not long after I was life professed I went to the Holy Cross monk who was then our superior and told him that I thought I had a contemplative vocation. In reply he quoted Father Whittemore, who had said a monastic should wait ten years after life profession before asking for a more contemplative lifestyle. That seemed sensible and I waited. More than ten years later, when we had our own superior, I told her this story, and asked if I might have a contemplative lifestyle—more time for prayer and less community responsibility and outside mission. Her answer was, "No way!" The community needed me at that time to keep on with the responsibilities I had. So I continued to work out my own balance of giving out and taking in. The "taking in" is for me a kind of holy "down time," "time out," a prayerful refilling with the Spirit when my spiritual tank seems empty. The "giving out" is the ministry which flows out of that.

In early Christian monasticism it seems that prayer and service were regarded as separate activities, if not opposing ones. Martha of Bethany exemplified the life of service and her sister Mary the life of contemplation, of sitting at Jesus' feet and listening. In our community we honor Mary's way by keeping the "great silence"— a time of no talking from sometime after the evening service of Compline until after morning prayers—and so those hours are available contemplative time. It was a breakthrough for me to realize I had four or five hours on both sides of sleep available for inner work and prayer, along with a brief rest period in the middle of the day. It came to me that that was how Jesus balanced his prayer and ministry: mostly praying when the day was over, and doing ministry steadily during "business hours." I begin to find that if I do use the hours after Compline and before breakfast as contemplative time, time with God to process my daily experience, I can work nonstop throughout the day and not get too much out of balance. It helps further that we have two retreat days a month that are silent days for the sisters, with no talking at meals and no meetings. Each sister may choose one of those days to *be* in retreat. Being in retreat does not mean having a day off. When I am in retreat at home I do some quiet work, do my share of dishwashing, go to chapel. We also have provisions for longer personal and community retreats. And we do have one "day off" a week, with no offices said and no meals served—we raid the kitchen for leftovers, do as much or little work as we choose, pray as much or little in whatever way we feel called.

With a much greater ability now to work at our own schedules than was true in the old days, when almost every activity had a built in timeframe—fifteen minutes for Bible reading, a half-hour twice a day for meditation—I find that work and prayer can flow together more smoothly. In addition, I have found that as my life goes on, the two modes become almost seamless. I can be more mindful and prayerful as I work. That reminds me of the old witticism about the Jesuit novice and his mentor. The young man asked the older one, "Father, can I smoke while I pray?" The old man replied, "Well, my son, I don't know, but you can surely pray while you smoke!"

When I am most in tune with the Holy Spirit I am hard-pressed to know moment by moment what is joy, prayer, ministry, and work. One day I was driving to a store on an errand ("work") for the household when I stopped at a red light. Suddenly the iridescence of the tiny glowing dots of brilliant red against the blue sky seemed beautiful beyond imagination. I was momentarily overcome by gratitude and a sense of the presence of God, lost in wonder, love, and praise. Then, of course, the light turned green, I came out of it, and went on my way. Was that errand work or prayer? The profundity of that moment has not happened since, but stopping at a red light now reminds me, and is an icon for, the knowledge of God's presence in my daily living. Sometimes I have this fuller sense of life even in going to tedious meetings or writing thank-you letters. In this same vein Brother Lawrence wrote that it was "a great delusion to imagine that prayer-time should be different from any other, for we are equally bound to be united to God by work at work-time as by prayer at prayer-time."[10]

A contemplative life in our world looks different from what it would have to Saint Teresa of Avila or Saint John of the Cross, and the life of Dag Hammarskjöld seems to me a fine example of a modern contemplative. Hammarskjöld was a Swedish diplomat and the second Secretary-General of the United Nations, exemplifying the man of action. But after his untimely death in a plane crash, his diary *Markings* was published. Begun when he was twenty years old and continued until his death, the diary reveals Hammarskjöld as a Christian mystic, and describes his diplomatic career as an inner journey. As this spiritual portrait reveals, in a mature person of prayer "inner and outer" dimensions of our lives do become integrated into one way of loving and serving. Although, as with almost anything in life, such accomplished integration is almost always the fruit of years of attention and practice.

One insight into the way that contemplation extends itself into ministry came to me when I was leading an adult study forum on spirituality at a large and sophisticated urban parish. In the question-and-answer time at the end of my talk, someone asked why I emphasized all the inner work of self-awareness and prayer. He wanted to know *what it was all for.* At that moment it felt as if the Holy Spirit dropped an answer into my head and I replied, "What all self-knowledge and all wisdom are *for* is to be given away. I have never had a baby, but my women friends tell me that when their breasts are full of milk, all they desire is for the baby to suck; for their child to take what they have been given. If the baby does not suck, it is very painful. In the same way if, like Mary of Bethany, we have through our attention to him been filled with the good milk of Jesus' message—the good news of spiritual freedom and peace—then we must give it away or else it becomes painful to us and others go hungry. But the baby must be ready to nurse. I've learned the hard way an important point for evangelism; it does no good, metaphorically, to pour a whole *pitcher* of milk over a baby's head! God invites us, never overwhelms us. As God's witness I try to be inviting and welcoming, so that people may ask and I may respond. All our gifts are meant to be given away, for others to take and receive and in turn offer us their gifts."

Despite this insight of ministry flowing out of contemplation, it has always been *easier* for me to practice the dimension of action rather than the contemplative one. I think that is why I have felt called to be contemplative—because my soul yearned to spend more time on the way that was hardest for me. When I feel I should stop and take a good look at something in my life, I still sometimes find it very hard to pay attention; it is easier to find something to *do*. Recently, for example, I woke up with a vague, uncomfortable feeling. To avoid paying attention to it and taking it into prayer, I did things: sorted out my credit card bill, ironed sacristy linens, ran an errand in the car that might have waited till later, and checked my email for the fourth time that day. Finally having run out of things to do, I sat down after Vespers to the hard work of giving attention to my feeling of unease, and I realized that I was angry. Anger is always hard for me to own up to, and until starting therapy in my forties I had thought of myself as even-tempered and "laid back"—nothing much ever bothered *me!* But then I began to remember my childhood temper tantrums and how, in response to my raging, my mother would lose patience and simply walk away. Soon I learned that any show of anger would result in abandonment by my mother. I have to remember over and over again why it is so hard for me to know that I am angry. Such close attention to the inner life takes real effort, and since mindfulness is so difficult, no wonder that many of us find activity more satisfying!

Another reason for choosing activity is that others can see the results and be grateful for what we've done. One day many years ago I became fully aware that my accomplishments were more readily rewarded than my attentive presence. It was after a hard day of spiritual conferences spent listening to people with profound and complex concerns. I received and held each of those concerns in my heart and in prayer, feeling privileged and glad to be invited into their spiritual journeys. But the listening and being present to each one of them had taken a lot out of me. It happened to be my turn that day to cook a simple supper for my household. I was thanked and complimented by several of my sisters for the soup I made; nobody thanked me for the much more taxing sitting and listening that I had done earlier that day.

The religious life aspires to be a balanced life, and the concept of balance carries with it the purpose of evening things up; not putting too much weight on one thing at the expense of another. I have wondered if this is why Jesus called Mary's way "the *better* part." Perhaps Jesus was here, as elsewhere, championing the less popular and more neglected way: the narrow gate and the hard road. In general we tend to disregard, if not criticize, sitting and listening. It is as if the conventional, if not parental, voice is saying, "Don't just sit there—get up and do something!" When paying attention seems hard, I often find myself ruefully remembering Scarlett O'Hara's great line, which might be a slogan for the easier way, "I'll think about that tomorrow!"

But the good news is that when contemplation and action have come into some kind of balance, I find that in the end both are equally needed, though at any given moment one or the other may be dominant. I have already used the human heart as a metaphor for the process of incorporation, but it can also be a metaphor for balance—without the even rhythm of systole and diastole, there is no life at all! Christians come together for prayer and go out to offer service, even though the ethos of any community—or the call of any individual—may emphasize one aspect or the other. This act of congregation and dispersion may be likened to the spiritual heartbeat, or the inhalation and exhalation of the breath of the body of Christ. The intake of breath is signified by Jesus' words to his disciples, "And I, when I am lifted up from the earth, will draw all people to myself" (John 12:32). Then the outflow of the Great Commission: "Go therefore and make disciples of all nations, baptizing them in the name of the Father and of the Son and of the Holy Spirit" (Matthew 28:19). On a profound level, prayer and work, *ora et labora,* together make up the life of the church.

However, in a community called to the mixed life, as we are, there may well be tension between those who feel called to a greater emphasis on prayer and those called to greater outreach and active ministry. Such tension, when experienced outside of a context of mutual respect, can become noxious. There is a tendency in life to polarize and eventually to disparage and belittle the other: "I am an active minister, you are only a contemplative." "I am a person of prayer, you are only a worker bee." "I am feeding all these people and you are just sitting there!" This labeling can be casual and benign, but unfortunately, if it is fed by insecurity and self-interest, it can grow into xenophobia and prejudice. The life of prayer, for instance, may be caricatured as nonproductive and navel-gazing; the active life as secular and self-serving. It is important to avoid placing such pejorative labels on differing choices of lifestyle because it is detrimental to the building up of the whole body in love.

On the other hand, creative and appropriate tension is what keeps the tightrope walker able to make the perilous journey. The middle of the tightrope is far less safe than the little platforms at either end. It is tempting to try to create two stable "platforms" and stand on one of them, avoiding the move out onto the rope. I have known a community that decided to become, if not formally "enclosed," then committed to staying at home and having no outreach. I have also heard of several religious congregations that have given up any chapel and community life, becoming instead a form of group housing for individual religious who were involved in full-time active ministries and who rarely ate, prayed, or enjoyed themselves together. Both of these ways were in a sense "platforms" to stand on, ways simpler to follow, but after a time they seemed to lose a sense of vitality and creative dynamism. A sister from another faith tradition once came to visit us and said, "Oh, I do envy you! You have kept the plainchant in choir and the common meal!"

Integrating contemplation and outreach require both flexibility and discipline. Discipline is not a good in itself, but only valuable if it is practiced in the cause of a greater good. When I fast, for example, that is not a good thing *in itself.* Sometimes I fast in order for the coming feast to be especially enjoyable; sometimes I fast to be in solidarity with Jesus' fasting; sometimes my fast is liturgical, as in Lent; and sometimes my abstinence is not fast at all, it is a way of dieting. The wrong understanding of discipline denies or represses desires and passions because they are bad, which in reality they are not. Human passions are integral to our nature and cannot be denied or repressed without grave consequence, but they can be disciplined and brought into balance. A wonderful metaphor for this ordering of the passions is attributed to Evagrius Ponticus, a fourth-century monk and hermit. The human passions, he proposed, are like a team of high-spirited horses harnessed to a chariot. The charioteer is the human will. If the will is weak, the horses will get the bits in their teeth and run away with the chariot; if the will is strengthened, all that horsepower can be employed to take the driver where he or she chooses to go. Practicing discipline is the way to make the will strong and free to choose for the best, and not to be driven.

Discipline, beauty, and balance have long held a significant place in monastic life. The art and architecture of our dwellings, the writing and illumination of manuscripts, the ancient music to which the psalms are chanted and the hymns sung—all offer to God our ordered praise. One might call it holy *feng shui,* after that practice, more than three thousand years old, of creating balanced, harmonious living and working space by the alignment of complementary opposites. Order and beauty in human surroundings, moreover, promote healing. One reason guests have said that common areas in monasteries and convents are restful and peaceful is that they are ordered so that no one's individual effects or clutter claim the space. The space belongs to God, and to each occupier of that space equally. We have one guest who says that whenever he comes back for retreat and enters our chapel, he can feel his blood pressure drop ten degrees.

Another reason for an atmosphere of peace lies in the even rhythm of prayer that pervades the atmosphere of our religious houses. At the center of the ordering of the monastic day—at its axis, I would say—is the Holy Eucharist. Even though it may not be as unique to the religious life as the daily office, the Eucharist is at the heart of monastic community. It was the first of four "marks" of early Christian groups, the others being community (koinonia), teaching (kerygma), and liturgy (liturgia). I would imagine there is not a second in the day when the Eucharist is not being celebrated somewhere on this earth. All Christians are called to this reenactment of the divine sacrifice of love, some of us weekly and most monastics daily. We come together in prayer and praise, we receive the bread and wine, and in the strength of that sustenance we go out in witness and ministry.

Another discipline important to monastic balance is the work of intercession—praying for others. Most monastic orders designate a time in chapel for community intercessions. In houses of the active or mixed life, intercessions may consist of five minutes before or within the daily office; in a contemplative order, it may mean almost continuous "shifts" of personal intercession in front of the reserved sacrament. In either case, intercession is an offering of prayer for all those friends and associates who have contacted the community in behalf of their own concerns or those of loved ones. And beyond that, there is remembrance of all suffering humanity, and the need for the peace and reordering of the world. In the convent where I live, we offer intercessions within the noonday office: after praying for some concerns aloud we remain together in silence for a time. I pray in the silence for those I know, and for all those whom I know only in spirit. I like to think of this exercise as my spirit and the Holy Spirit and all the saints in heaven joining in mutual care. Many people have asked me if I pray to the saints. I don't pray to them as I pray to God, but as if the church on earth is a seamless whole with the church in heaven. If I intercede to holy women and men in heaven, it is just as if I asked of one of my earthly friends, "Please pray with me for my sister who has just had an ominous biopsy report."

We pray for our associates aloud in chapel, daily in rotation. They are men and women who are in some way drawn to the monastic life, but because of other commitments and a different calling do not choose, or are not free, to live the vowed life in community. They desire a connection with a religious community and for themselves a modified rule of life. The Franciscans call such persons a "third order," while other communities have companions and oblates. Some of our associates live halfway around the world and are connected mainly by mutual prayer, correspondence, and through our newsletter and website; others are neighbors who come regularly to pray with us in chapel and share a meal, and sometimes help us in our work. These relationships are a significant way in which we can balance and share our lives as religious with the larger community of the church and the world.

Perceiving the whole body of Christ as intimately and organically connected, as both temporal and eternal, we can understand why there is truth in the statement that there is no such thing as "private" prayer. And yet, paradoxically, each of us is called to pray individually, seeking to join his or her human spirit with the Holy Spirit in love. And then, as I am sustained by prayer, I go out to witness, serve, and minister. To seek the truth in contemplation and then to witness to that truth. There is never, of course, any guarantee that what I give will be received, or that what I speak will be heard. If Jesus was not heard by so many people, especially in his home-town and among his own family, how will people hear any one of us? I think it is an old Zen saying that if a teacher has, at the end of a long life of teaching, one dis-ciple—one person who really *gets it*—that teacher is for-tunate! We are only responsible for trying to present what we have been given so that it may be heard; we are not responsible for creating the ears that can hear.

Balance is integral to a healthy and holy life, but it is, in a sense, always tenuous. Each experience that comes to me, each choice I make, tips the scales of my life jour-ney one way or the other: toward a life of activity or toward a life of prayer. When I used to facilitate a work-shop model called "community building," we had pens made up with an old refrain from a Frank Sinatra song: "Do be do be do be do be do!" But for me, in a way, the integration of doing and being seems not to be so much an equal division of prayer and ministry as one *proceed-ing* from the other. As Father J.O.S.H. Huntington wrote in his rule for the Order of the Holy Cross, which is part of my own community's history, "Though our vocation as an order is to the mixed life, active and contemplative, yet the contemplative is that which alone can vivify and supernaturalize the active." That is my goal, but mentally and emotionally I am still usually off-balance in the being and doing department, as perhaps everyone is. I knew a young monk once who said, "I don't need to pray, my whole life is a prayer." Well, it didn't look that way to me! It seems to me that integration comes at the end of a lifetime's practice and not before—at least that is how I think it will be for me.

Like the practice of prayer and contemplation, that part of my life in community called ministry has also been a practice—an evolution, a journey. My idea of ministry and my practice of it is very different now than when I was a novice. The development of my ministry was a very gradual thing. I don't now see it as a case of trial and *error,* but it was surely a case of trial and reevaluation. (I think maybe our life choices are never really errors. It is very hard *deliberately* to choose what will be bad for us!) But if a certain ministry didn't work out well, or didn't last, I have had to reevaluate and try another direction.

At one time I loved the work of campus ministry and the collegiality and teamwork it involved—I thought it was just the right thing for me. But when that mission was over, there was another ministry awaiting me. I was asked to preach and to lead retreats, quiet days, and Lenten programs, all of which required me to write and talk on spiritual themes. Then I said to myself. "Aha! *This* is my life ministry! I am to go around talking about spirituality—be essentially what is called a retreat conductor. This is my niche in life!" Then more people started coming to the convent to talk to me about spiritual things and I thought, "No, essentially I am a spiritual director." About this time I served for several years on the staff of the newly founded program for spiritual direction at Vancouver School of Theology in British Columbia. Then after a few years I moved back from the West Coast to our convent in New York, and my work in spiritual direction dwindled, though it has never completely ceased. Then, for more than twelve years I was a facilitator for weekend workshops run on a model created by psychotherapist M. Scott Peck, facilitating workshops in America, Canada, Britain, and as far away as Belize, Pakistan, and Sri Lanka. I said to myself, "Well, this is my *ultimate* ministry!" When that declined, a decade of leadership in my own community followed and *that* seemed my ultimate call. I am now retired from community responsibilities—so now what is my ministry? I feel I have come to a place where it doesn't much matter what I choose to do, or am called to do—there is a whole world out there, as well as here in the convent, to be ministered to in any number of ways. Maybe my ministry now is writing. I have written since I was twelve years old, and perhaps, like the bluebird of happiness, writing has been waiting for me all this time to be rediscovered in my own backyard.

But in the end, my true core ministry is simply *being*. That to me is very freeing. Even more importantly, I have come to realize that I do not need a ministry to define me; nothing I do will really define who I am or add to or detract from my being.

When I try to open my mind to new ways of ordering my life, I am constantly challenged to let go of old ingrained concepts and opinions. I begin to understand why in earlier times monastic novices were told to plant cabbages upside down and to water dry sticks. These actions were against all reason, opposed to all logic, and therefore exercised the mind and will to be open to contradiction, to have less need for having things "the way they have always been," or the way my ego could control them. I think now that such exercises were meant to free the right side of the brain. Presumably this is also the intention behind the Zen practice of using the *koan* as a teaching device, as in: "Think of the sound of one hand clapping." I will defend to the death our call to think logically and to use God's great gift of reason, but I also have learned to allow my best logic to be surrendered to paradox, and beyond that to mystery. As Methodist theologian Ray Hart once wrote, "We are invited into knowledge, but received into mystery."

All our lives are received into God's divine mystery. The religious life is no different from any other in this respect. I have said that the religious life is an intense life, and has as much difficulty and stress as any other way of living. But it can be a life of profound meaning, fulfillment, and joy. It has been, and continues to be so, for me.

Notes

1. Laura Swan, *The Forgotten Desert Mothers: Sayings, Lives and Stories of Early Christian Women* (Mahwah, N.J.: Paulist Press, 2001), 43.

2. Teresa of Avila, *The Complete Works of Saint Teresa of Avila: Way of Perfection,* ed. E. Allison Peers (New York: Sheed and Ward, 1946), 69.

3. Evelyn Underhill, *The Spiritual Life* (London: Hodder and Stoughton, 1937), 24.

4. *The Earlier Rule of Saint Francis,* in *Francis and Clare: The Complete Works,* trans. Regis J. Armstrong, OFM Cap, The Classics of Western Spirituality (New York: Paulist Press, 1982), 113.

5. W. H. Longridge, SSJE, *Ignatian Retreats* (London: A. R. Mowbray, 1926), 122.

6. Aelred of Rievaulx, *Spiritual Friendship* (Kalamazoo: Cistercian Publications, 1977), 72.

7. Introduction to Aelred, *Spiritual Friendship,* 21–22.

8. Dietrich Bonhoeffer, *Life Together* (New York: Harper and Row, 1954), 27.

9. Saint Benedict, *Rule for Monastics* (Collegeville, Minn.: The Liturgical Press, 1947), 12–13.

10. Brother Lawrence, *The Practice of the Presence of God,* trans. Donald Atwater (Springfield, Ill.: Templegate, 1974), 49.